How to Heal After Heartbreak

How to Recover from a Breakup
and Get Your Hopes and Dreams Back

Chris Gotts

HOW TO HEAL AFTER HEARTBREAK: HOW TO RECOVER FROM A BREAKUP AND GET YOUR HOPES AND DREAMS BACK

Copyright © 2014 Atlantic Publishing Group, Inc.
1405 SW 6th Avenue • Ocala, Florida 34471 • Phone 800-814-1132 • Fax 352-622-1875
Website: www.atlantic-pub.com • E-mail: sales@atlantic-pub.com
SAN Number: 268-1250

Library of Congress Cataloging-in-Publication Data

Gottschalk, Christopher, 1976-
  How to heal after heartbreak : how to recover from a breakup and get your hopes and dreams back / by Chris Gottschalk.
    p. cm.
  Includes bibliographical references and index.
  ISBN-13: 978-1-60138-583-3 (alk. paper)
  ISBN-10: 1-60138-583-8 (alk. paper)
  1. Couples. 2. Separation (Psychology) 3. Adjustment (Psychology) 4. Self-help techniques. 5. Interpersonal relations. I. Title.
  HQ801.G5985 2010
  646.7'7--dc22
                              2010039863

Printed on Recycled Paper

Printed in the United States

INTERIOR LAYOUT: Antoinette D'Amore • addesign@videotron.ca
COVER DESIGNS: Jackie Miller • millerjackiej@gmail.com

A few years back we lost our beloved pet dog Bear, who was not only our best and dearest friend but also the "Vice President of Sunshine" here at Atlantic Publishing. He did not receive a salary but worked tirelessly 24 hours a day to please his parents.

Bear was a rescue dog who turned around and showered myself, my wife, Sherri, his grandparents Jean, Bob, and Nancy, and every person and animal he met (well, maybe not rabbits) with friendship and love. He made a lot of people smile every day.

We wanted you to know a portion of the profits of this book will be donated in Bear's memory to local animal shelters, parks, conservation organizations, and other individuals and nonprofit organizations in need of assistance.

– Douglas & Sherri Brown

PS: We have since adopted two more rescue dogs: first Scout, and the following year, Ginger. They were both mixed golden retrievers who needed a home.

Want to help animals and the world? Here are a dozen easy suggestions you and your family can implement today:

- *Adopt and rescue a pet from a local shelter.*
- *Support local and no-kill animal shelters.*
- *Plant a tree to honor someone you love.*
- *Be a developer — put up some birdhouses.*
- *Buy live, potted Christmas trees and replant them.*
- *Make sure you spend time with your animals each day.*
- *Save natural resources by recycling and buying recycled products.*
- *Drink tap water, or filter your own water at home.*
- *Whenever possible, limit your use of or do not use pesticides.*
- *If you eat seafood, make sustainable choices.*
- *Support your local farmers market.*
- *Get outside. Visit a park, volunteer, walk your dog, or ride your bike.*

Five years ago, Atlantic Publishing signed the Green Press Initiative. These guidelines promote environmentally friendly practices, such as using recycled stock and vegetable-based inks, avoiding waste, choosing energy-efficient resources, and promoting a no-pulping policy. We now use 100-percent recycled stock on all our books. The results: in one year, switching to post-consumer recycled stock saved 24 mature trees, 5,000 gallons of water, the equivalent of the total energy used for one home in a year, and the equivalent of the greenhouse gases from one car driven for a year.

Acknowledgements

Authors get a lot of support while writing a book, and I am no exception. Thanks to my family, who in addition to being lovely people were there for me when I had my heart broken and have supported me in trying to be a writer, neither of which is easy to do. These things mean a lot.

Thanks to the people who took the time to submit case studies and those friends who suggested different sources for the book. It was a huge help, even if the sources did not end up being used.

Also deserving of thanks are my editors — Kim Fulscher, Angela Pham, and Shannon McCarthy — who kept the book on target, argued with me over changes, and graciously granted me extensions on deadlines, particularly at the end.

Table of Contents

Contents

Chapter 3: The Disengagement Protocols

Chapter 4: The Ex Games

Chapter 5: How to Not
Let Yourself Go Mentally........................ 127

Chapter 6: How to Not Let Yourself Go Physically......................153

Chapter 7: Getting Support From Others 169

Chapter 10: Finding and Meeting New People 229

Chapter 11: Meeting Your Match Online 259

How to Have a Healthy Breakup

E ven if breaking up is the right thing to do, it is not easy. Here are some tips that can help you get through your breakup, no matter what side you are on:

- **You can cry.** Even if you think of yourself as tough, the emotional pain you are going through can bring anyone to tears. You might also want to contact a friend or family member to offer you a literal shoulder on which to cry. You need to accept that it is fine to feel bad about the dissolution of your relationship.

- **Find new things to do.** Now is the time to take the art class you have been thinking about or try to make your way through *War and Peace*. Maybe you can enroll in a tae kwon do class or join a hockey team. Being depressed makes you want to sit around and mope, but resist the urge. The more you are active, the more things you will find to fill the emotional hole your ex left.

- **Talk to other people.** Try not to wear out your friends and family, but do not keep your feelings to yourself. Talk to other people and get those feelings off your chest. However, you will want to watch what you say, especially if you have mutual friends. You can talk about how you feel the relationship was not working, but do not distort your ex. Be as honest as possible.

- **Be optimistic.** Do not give in to the negative feelings you experience during a break up. Instead of dwelling on the past relationship, look forward to the next one instead. If you alter the way you think, you can change the way you feel, which will change the way you act. When you finally feel optimistic, you can free yourself to accomplish new goals, try new things, and start to live life to its fullest again.

Introduction

If you are reading this book, you are likely getting over a recent bout of heartbreak. Also likely is that, whatever happened, it was painful. Perhaps your relationship dissolved in one huge fight. Perhaps it just faded slowly, until you and your partner woke up one morning and discovered that after 15 years, you did not love each other anymore. Maybe your partner said one final, hateful remark that burrowed its way into your psyche and kicked down your self-confidence. Maybe you two tried to end on good terms and promised, that no matter what, you would remain friends.

Regardless, you are likely alone now. Depending on the time frame, you could still be at the stage in which you have inadvertently memorized the television schedule. Or you could be out, going to your job, buying groceries, and acting as though everything is alright. Chances are, you have friends who have also had their share of heartbreak, and you might be thinking of them

and remembering how they were sad before they were out having drinks with you and other friends. You are wondering if they
were that well adjusted or if they are like you and put on a brave
front. You might even try to convince yourself you are alright and
rebound into another relationship but still think of your ex.

Whatever your situation, getting your heart broken is painful.
Dealing with that sudden void where someone special used to be
is not easy, and even people who seem to get past the depression
heartbreak causes still find themselves with periods where they
are reminded they used to be in a relationship. During a weak
moment, you might wonder whether you will ever get over this
heartbreak and get on with your life again.

That is where this book comes in. You will receive help on how to
get through your breakup and the resulting heartbreak, and how
to recover your life again as you emerge with renewed hopes
and dreams.

We will start with the dissolution of the relationship and will
discuss the stages of how a relationship ends and map out what
happens at each stage. We will also take a look at the methods
people use when they break up. That will lead us to where we
look at the Five Stages of Loss — denial, anger, bargaining, depression, and acceptance — and talk about how you can deal
with each one. From there is a guide on how to disengage yourself from your ex. You will learn the best way to separate yourself, the excuses you make to see your ex again and why they are
not good ideas, and how to share news of the breakup with your

family and friends. Because this is the 21st century, we will also cover the tricky subject of dealing with your breakup on social media sites.

You will likely have to be around your ex at some point. You might have similar social circles and might still share friends. You might even have had children together. Because you might have conflicting ideas on how to behave, Chapter 4 will cover how to be on your best behavior and why that is important, and will show you unhealthy behaviors to avoid. Because you might have an ex who has no compunctions about being on his or her best behavior, this chapter will also cover how to handle an ex who is behaving badly or in ways that make you worry about your mental or physical well-being. Also, because one of the common goals of heartbreak victims is to preserve the friendship, this chapter will discuss the benefits and drawbacks of trying to be friends with your ex with the goal most separated couples eventually consider — reconciling with each other.

You will also need to keep busy after you have broken up with someone, so you will learn how to fill the void your ex left in your life. This chapter will explain why you need to keep busy and features a comprehensive overview of how to figure out what you want to do, even if you feel like doing nothing. Chapters 6 and 7 will discuss how to maintain yourself physically and mentally. Diet, exercise, and positive thinking will be covered.

The support of your friends and family is also a way to cope with your heartbreak. You will initially find out how to get support from your friends and your family, and how to do so without wearing them down. You will also find out about online support groups and websites that might help you cope with your feelings. Perhaps most important though will be the topic of when to seek professional health. This chapter will cover determining the point when you need to seek professional help, what to expect in therapy, and how to find a suitable therapist. Because you might be placed in group therapy as part of your treatment, you will also learn how it works and how to behave.

Most breakups take their toll on a person's self-confidence and self-esteem. Chapter 9 will talk about how to restore your self-confidence. You will find out how to talk positively to yourself and how to avoid the negativity traps that devour people. Because you will feel vulnerable to the opinions of others at this point, you will get some advice on how to ignore personal attacks other people might direct at you.

Some breakups, however, are not just about you and your ex. You might also have children to consider. This book has a chapter devoted to single parents dealing with breakups and heartbreak. It starts with telling your children that you and your ex are breaking up, then covers some practical matters, such as how to handle child care and child support, how to move past the stigma of being a single parent, and how to improve your time-planning strategies to ensure you and your children get the family time you need while giving yourself the "me" time you deserve. This chapter will also help you figure out how to deal with your ex, especially in front of the children. You will also get some advice on how to introduce a new partner to children, including when it is time to introduce them.

After you have weathered the worst of your heartbreak, you can start to think about regaining your hopes and dreams. The first thing you will need to do is take stock of your life and set some goals, and in Chapter 11 you will learn how by finding out the areas in which you are happy and the areas on which you want to work. Because organizing your thoughts is a key step in taking stock of your life, this chapter will also show you how to create lists. You will get guidelines on how to make lists that are useful to you and advice on how to thoroughly analyze and realize on what you want to work.

Once you have taken stock of your life, you can start to set goals. You will learn how to ensure your goals are realistic, then figure out the first steps that will put you on your way to achieving those goals.

Chapter 12 focuses on finding and meeting new people. You will find ideas on where to look for new friendships or relationships. If you are determined to find someone new in a different way, advice about online dating, speed dating, and singles' nights are provided. Because not everyone is gifted in the art of chatting people up, a crash course in how to strike up a conversation and keep it going is provided. This section culminates in one of the most perennially difficult parts of any new relationship — asking out the other person.

Asking out another person means you are ready to begin a new relationship, and that is what the final chapter will cover. You will learn when is the right time to move on, why you should not start your search for a romantic partner too soon, and what problems can arise in rebound relationships. Perhaps most important, you will learn how to avoid sabotaging your new relationship, such as raising your standards too high and why to not compare your new boyfriend or girlfriend with your ex.

You can also rest comfortably knowing that someone who has also experienced serious heartbreak will be guiding you through this process. Speaking as the author, I have had my share of heartbreak, which felt less like a roadblock on the road to happiness and more like a sledgehammer to the forehead. I recall trying everything to get over heartbreak, from getting out and doing something to writing bad poetry to being curled up in a ball in front of the television for days.

But enough talking — it is time to get to business. Get yourself something nice to drink and a comfort snack or two. Then sit down in your favorite reading spot, and turn to Chapter 1.

BUT MY RELATIONSHIP IS DIFFERENT!

Most of the time, books that offer relationship advice talk about getting over relationships from the viewpoint of a girlfriend getting over a boyfriend, or a boyfriend getting over a girlfriend. But what if you are not in that kind of relationship? Will this book help you, too?

This book is for you, no matter what kind of relationship you have, and regardless of whether you are heterosexual, homosexual, bisexual, male, or female. Maybe your marriage of seven years is ending; maybe you are becoming single in your 50s or 60s. Or maybe it was the end of an intense college relationship. You may be looking at this book and wondering if it will even offer you any advice you can use. Rest assured, this book is built for you, no matter what your relationship. No matter how different you think your relationship might be, human beings go through similar reactions and stages. Loss is universal. So is recovering from it. No matter how far along you were in your relationship when you got your heart broken or what kind of relationship it was, there is something in this book for you. Believe it or not, we are all in this together.

Chapter 1

Understanding How a Relationship Fails

Getting your heart broken raises questions. Why did he or she leave? What could I have done to prevent this? Will I ever see the stuff I left at his or her place again?

One common question, though, is, "How did this happen?" People try to figure out how their relationship fell apart, and the question cannot be answered. Researchers Steve Duck and Julia Wood studied the process of falling out of love in 2006 and 2007. Out of their studies, they came up with what they call the "Death Cycle of Relationships," a corollary of sorts to their model of the stages involved in building up a relationship.

While friendships might end in different ways, the process of falling out of love is consistent.

Falling out of love starts with a phase called the **intrapsychic processes**, in which one or both people in the relationship are aware of the relationship's problems. During this phase, focusing on the relationship's negative parts might lead to more negative thoughts about the relationship. In time, this affects the person's outlook of the relationship. The intrapsychic stage is also when the people in the relationship begin thinking about other relationships they could be having. This is the stage where you start to feel his or her constant lateness is less of a cute personality quirk and more of a sign that he or she feels your relationship is less of a priority than his or her projects. This is where you start to realize that when he or she teases you in front of your friends, he or she is being mean.

CONFLICT IN ROMANTIC RELATIONSHIPS

One of the worst ways to break up with someone is to say something in the middle of a fight that you cannot take back. The better you are at handling conflict, the smoother your relationship will be, and if you do have to break up with your partner, you can take comfort in the knowledge that you handled your conflict well, even if you do not end up together. To that end, here is quick advice to help you constructively handle those conflicts that indicate something is wrong with your relationship.

Before the discussion:

- Before you begin talking with your partner about a conflict, calm down. Talking about the conflict when you are upset or angry can result in destructive communication and regret afterward.

- Make sure your partner is ready to discuss the problem with you. If your significant other does not want to talk, no constructive communication can arise.

- Schedule time to talk about the conflict. Give yourself time or set up time to cool down.

- After you have scheduled a time for the discussion, know your goal. It might be nice to win the argument, but you do not want your partner to feel like he or she has lost.

- Find out what your partner's goal is in this discussion.

- Plan to discuss the conflict in a private place. No one likes seeing couples argue publicly, least of all the couple themselves.

- Plan to have enough time to properly discuss the conflict because it is hard to give your full attention to something when you have an impending deadline or appointment.

During the discussion:

- Frame the discussion in a way that each person gains something. Think about what you want to get out of the discussion and how your partner can benefit from it. For instance, if you want your partner to be more punctual, you can frame your goal by saying, "I wish you would not be late for our dates. The later you are for a date, the less time we can spend together. It also seems to make us stressed, which detracts from the time we spend together. Is there a way we can work to increase your punctuality and decrease the stress in both our lives?"

- Listen to what your partner says. At first, do not try to launch a counterargument. Understand his or her point of view, and be sure to convey that you are listening to what he or she is saying.

- To let your partner know you are listening, calmly paraphrase his or her arguments. Your partner will be happy that you seem to understand what he or she has to say, and this technique is a way to force yourself to process your partner's statements. Keep your tone non-condescending and non-judgmental.

When you get a chance to talk, use words that show you value the other person and that you want to cooperate with him or her. For instance, you can say, "I think we should..." or "You have a point." Also, use "I" statements to convey how you feel instead of blame-placing "you" statements. Instead of saying, "You do not respect me when you make me wait for a long time," say, "I feel that you do not respect my time when you are late and I have gone to the effort of being on time."

Resolve the conflict:

- Value everyone involved in the conflict and their points of contention. This includes you and your partner and the relationship itself.

- To manage the conflict so it can be constructive, validate how your partner feels. If you find out what is causing her to be late, you can come up with a solution that will not make her feel insulted but will make you feel you have made your feelings known.

The way you handle this conflict will strengthen the relationship as you set new parameters and learn more about each other. Perhaps you agree to give him or her a 20-minute warning call on his or her cellphone, or he or she agrees to call you a half-hour before you are scheduled to meet. The best conclusion is where you feel respected.

If you do not value or understand your partner's point of view, it can lead to a bad outcome. You might slip into a "win-lose" scenario, in which you want to win the conflict. In this case, it would be forcing him or her to be punctual by harping on his or her perceived immaturity and irresponsibility, followed up by threats of doing things by yourself and not inviting him or her if he or she is going to be late. You might win the conflict and get your partner to be punctual, but he or she will be aware he or she has lost the conflict. That, and the relationship has changed. You have established yourself as the more dominant force in this conflict, and you have shown your partner that you see your views as paramount. This is alright as long as your partner does not have the same view.

If your partner feels as strongly about the issue as you do, the scenario can deteriorate into a lose-lose. In this scenario, you walk away unsatisfied. The issue is unlikely to be resolved, and even if it is, the relationship itself is damaged because neither of you walk away feeling your opinions matter to the other person.

Gracefulness is another important part of valuing all aspects of the relationship. Show grace after conflicts, especially when you are in the right. If your partner admits he or she was in the wrong and wants to work with you to correct his or her behavior, work with him or her and then put the incident behind you. For instance, if you have had a conflict with your partner about not cleaning the kitchen after every meal and he or she agrees this is a problem, do not harp on his or her previous failure by saying, "We need to clean the kitchen after dinner," or, "Do I need to remind you to clean the kitchen?" If you are going to say anything, say, "Let's clean the kitchen and then watch TV," or "Need help cleaning the kitchen?" If you want to be graceful, clean the kitchen by yourself if he forgets. Displaying thoughtfulness and forgiveness can go a long way in showing your commitment to a relationship, and in this scenario, your partner is likely to be touched by the gesture. Grace is not appropriate. You do not want your partner to take advantage of you, after all.

If the problems the intrapsychic processes unearthed are not solved, the exclusive nature of the relationship — complete with inside jokes and communication shortcuts — begins to deteriorate. At this point, the decay of the relationship moves into the **dyadic process**. This is one of the important points of a relationship breakdown because couples start to neglect areas of their relationship they once maintained. These areas involve communication. Because women tend to become less happy with a relationship the more communication in the relationship deteriorates, this stage can be detrimental to women. The dyadic process affects men because men become unhappy in a relationship when treasured routines and behaviors go away. This is from where the clichéd phrase, "We do not talk anymore" comes.

The dyadic process stage is when each partner should be aware that there are problems with the relationship. According to Steve Duck's research, these problems get addressed. This is the stage at which the relationship can be saved, but the people involved must be willing to discuss the rough spots in their relationship (in other words, address the issues), possess the ability to communicate enough with each other to understand each other's problems, and be committed enough to save the relationship. If the relationship cannot be saved, the relationship fails, and each partner must deal with the final stages on his or her own.

During the **social support** stage, each person in the relationship turns to other people for support as their relationship collapses. People look to their relatives — their immediate family — or their friends. This is the stage of the breakup that draws in other people. These outside friends dread their involvement in a breakup between two friends like Ulysses dreaded sailing between Scylla and Charybdis. The reason is that during this stage of the relationship breakdown, each person in the former relationship desires — perhaps even needs — sympathy and support from other people. People in a dissolving relationship might also want to avoid being embarrassed by their actions or thoughts before the breakup; as a result, both parties portray themselves in the best possible light. They might also succumb to the temptation of giving less-than-flattering accounts of their exes, regardless of how it might come back to haunt them in the future. This stage can be wearisome for mutual friends of the former couple because the friends feel pressured to choose between one person and the other. This results in the loss of a friend. This is especially true when relationships between married couples end because married couples share the same set of friends.

After the talking has been done and the issues have been pondered, each member of the relationship is finally ready for the second-to-last phase in the relationship's death. The **grave-dressing process** is named such because at this point, people bury the relationship and start to accept its loss. Mourning is common at this point, and almost everyone is introspective to a degree, pondering the wonderful parts of the relationship and perhaps even imagining what might have been. Although this kind of reflection can be seen as a refusal to move on with your life, it is considered healthy, provided the reflective period does not last so long that people start to dwell on their thoughts. According to studies James Honeycutt in 2003 and Colleen Saffrey and Marion Ehrenberg in 2007 conducted, the more you reflect on your breakup, the more likely you are to cause someone to become depressed and deal with the break up more negatively than someone who only reflects on the former relationship for a little while and then moves on.

The final part of the relationship death cycle is a happy one. The **resurrection process** is when both people are "reborn" and consider themselves single again. They are able to move on with their lives. They begin to reorganize their lives to compensate for the loss of the ex-partner, and they start to do things as a single person and even look to establish another romantic connection.

 MIX-AND-MATCH STRATEGIES

Throughout the breakup strategies discussed, you might be replaying the events of your breakup in your mind and trying to discover the strategy used to exit your relationship. Do not be surprised if the method used in your relationship does not resemble one strategy.

People use multiple strategies to break up with someone. They switch strategies to make their point. For instance, if a woman uses the **avoidance** strategy, she might go for the **direct dump** when her boyfriend spots her in the supermarket and confronts her about her behavior. Other times, they might adjust their strategies based on the reaction of the other person, such as when an ex begins to cry during the justification strategy and the dumper switches to the **positive tone** strategy to make the ex feel better.

Breakup Strategies

A common reaction to heartbreak is to try to figure out what happened. Why did he list all the things I did wrong when he did not make a big deal out of them before? Why was she nice to me and tell me what a good guy I was before leaving forever? Did he think not seeing me for two weeks was a relationship-ending strategy? Although cataloging the mindset of every couple that breaks up is impossible, determining how someone broke up with you is easier and might shed some light on the things your ex did when he or she broke up with you.

Despite what Paul Simon claims, there are only about 13 ways to leave your lover. Each of these strategies falls into one of four categories, based on two conditions, according to one of the premier researchers in the field of breaking up, Leslie A. Baxter. According to her research, the first condition is who wants out of the relationship. If the breakup is initiated because one person wants out of the relationship, then the breakup is considered **unilateral**. Less common is that both people in the relationship realize they are no longer interested in maintaining the relationship. This is a **bilateral** breakup.

The second condition is whether the breakup will be **direct** or **indirect**. This is the part that draws interest from people because it determines how the breakup will occur. The indirect method of breaking up can take different forms. This might be accomplished by completely shutting down all forms of communication, including not answering telephone calls and ignoring e-mail. Or, the person who wants the breakup might leave subtle hints, such as reducing affection down to the occasional hug or going out with friends instead of spending time with his or her partner, in the hopes that the other person picks up on the hints. Then there is the direct method of breaking up. Unlike the indirect method, the direct method is straightforward and hard, if not impossible, to misunderstand. Tell the other person point-blank that you are breaking up with him or her. Decide that given the problems you are having, it is time to end the relationship and put everything into a "State of the Relationship" speech. Or just state that the relationship is done, without giving any reason why.

These conditions and methods combine in four ways, with each way having different approaches.

Bilateral indirect strategies

This has only one strategy associated with it — the **fadeaway**.

THE FADEAWAY

[Silence]

This is a quiet way of breaking up, when the couple grows apart. This is common during long-distance relationships, and during a fadeaway, a talk about the relationship might not be necessary; the couple might sense the relationship is over. This is the type of situation where the hot guy you made out with at basket-ball camp just fades from memory, even though the two of you promised you would see each other again. It could also be when, after calls to your boyfriend in graduate school, you realize that keeping in touch with him becomes less frequent. So when you find someone else to date, calling your boyfriend to break up is just a formality.

Bilateral direct strategies

A breakup where both people feel the relationship needs to end has two strategies associated with it.

THE BLAME GAME

"You're such a slob — I can't believe you haven't killed me with germs."

"Just go ahead and yell at me. I guess that's what you're best at."

"I don't know why I ever thought you were worth dating."

"Same here."

In the **blame game,** partners shift the responsibility for the dying relationship onto each other and blame the other person for the relationship's death. This continues after the relationship has ended because even the reasons the relationship has ended are argued over. This type of breakup can get extremely messy, and the people in the relationship rarely end with positive feelings toward each other. However, this strategy provides each partner with a reason to end the relationship, and blaming the end of the relationship on the other person helps each side not have to admit he or she might have been at fault, letting him or her save face.

THE NEGOTIATED BREAKUP

"This isn't working."

"No...it's not. I'm sorry."

"Me too. We're going to have to figure out who gets what, though. I think one of us should get the big-screen TV, and the other should get the video game console."

"That sounds fair, but could the person who gets the video game console chip in for another copy of a video game?"

"How about a used copy?"

"We can do that."

A healthier breakup strategy is what Baxter names the **negotiated farewell**. This strategy is similar to the blame game because both sides realize the relationship has what Hollywood couples refer to as "irreconcilable differences." Instead of blaming the other person, however, the partners instead negotiate how to leave the relationship, with each person wanting to be as fair to the other person as possible. The goal of couples engaged in the negotiated farewell is to leave the relationship on a high note, with positive feelings toward each other. Issues covered might be how to split possessions, how to coexist with each other in social circles, and even how to figure out the best way to resolve child custody. Only couples that have been intimate for a long time or in a long-term, committed relationship use this technique.

HOW LONG IS A LONG TIME?

In the negotiated farewell strategy of leaving, you might be asking yourself, "How long is a long time?" When someone is involved in a long-term relationship, how long is that? The answer is hard to define. A reliable definition, though, is when two people have been together long enough to reach the stage of a relationship known as "emotional attachment," according to researcher Helen Fisher at Rutgers University. Unlike the "romantic feelings" stage of the relationship, when your heart and hormones run wild, and the "physical attraction" stage, known as being lovesick, the emotional attachment stage is when you realize your partner is not perfect, and the good outweighs the bad. Reaching this stage does not happen immediately, nor does it happen at the same pace. But as a rule of thumb, a relationship that has lasted for one year or longer is a long-term relationship.

Unilateral indirect strategies

When one person wants to get out of a relationship and does not want the potential confrontation that can ignite during a breakup talk, they might employ one of three potential strategies.

AVOIDANCE

"I'd love to spend time with you, but I just can't. I've got a project I have to work on that's making me put in overtime, then I have to visit my parents, and after that I promised my brother I'd help him move. I know I haven't talked to you in the past week. Sorry. Goodbye."

The **avoidance** strategy is simple. Avoid him or her and shut down all lines of communication. The idea is that when your partner sees you are actively avoiding all attempts at talking with him or her, he or she will understand the relationship has ended and get on with life. This breakup strategy is used when one person simply wants to end the relationship and does not foresee any friendship with the other person in the future. Additionally, it is used more in low-intimacy relationships, when the people in the relationship have few formal ties to each another, and when the person breaking up does not have a positive opinion of his or her partner. But this strategy rarely works as well as the person doing it would hope. Avoidance presumes that your soon-to-be ex understands you perfectly or that he or she can read your mind. If your partner does not hear from you, he or she is more likely to want to find out why you have not talked to him or her than he or she is to understand you want to break up. Eventually, the person doing the breaking up will have to say something to get the point across.

COST ESCALATION

"I spent the $20 that was on your nightstand on the movie we were supposed to see Friday. And you need to go out grocery shopping because I drank the last of the milk. Could you throw the carton away, too?"

Another strategy is called **cost escalation**. This entails worsening your behavior by becoming meaner and more inconsiderate to your partner, thereby making him or her think favorably of breaking up with you. This is the least used of all break-up strategies. Ironically, this can be beneficial to both parties in the relationship. When the person whom you are trying to break up with breaks up with you first, the relationship ends with both sides feeling better about the choice they made to end the relationship. Your ex feels he or she got out of a relationship that was steadily worsening, and you do not have to live with the guilt of breaking his or her heart.

PSEUDO DE-ESCALATION

"I'm just saying we should be friends, not boyfriend and girl-friend. There have been difficulties, and they weren't there when we were friends. So if we go back to being friends, we can still be happy without getting on each other's nerves."

The final unilateral indirect strategy is **pseudo de-escalation**. This indirect method of breaking up is when one partner tries to de-escalate the relationship from romantic to platonic, or at least to not being as close as they were before. This can be anything from a "let's just be friends" speech to "let's take a break from the relationship" speech.

Unilateral direct strategies

DIRECT DUMP

"I want to break up."

This is more familiar territory. One person wants out of the rela-tionship, and he or she expresses problems and concerns to the other person. At its core, the **direct dump** strategy sums up the unilateral direct strategy. This approach is when one person in a relationship approaches the other and announces that he or she wants to end the relationship. The person using the direct dump will have an argument as to why the breakup is preferable to remaining in the relationship and offer the other person no choice but to agree to end the relationship. According to Baxters' research, 81 percent of the people who were broken up with using the direct dump accepted the breakup without putting up a fight, which suggests the advantage of using such a strong message. However, this strategy can be rough for the person on the receiving end because he or she suddenly is told the relationship has ended and has no choice in the matter. The direct dump is used after other, more subtle break-up strategies have failed.

JUSTIFICATION

"When we first got together, we were in college; we both wanted to go to graduate school and we had the same interests. But we've both changed. You didn't get into graduate school and worked as an IT manager, and I'm involved with getting my medical degree. You're more interested in video games, and I joined that book club. We don't talk about anything anymore, and you're not interested in being more mature, and I'm just too involved in medicine to be romantic with someone right now. Do you see why I think we should break up?"

The **justification** strategy is similar to the direct dump, but with justification, the person breaking up explains to the other person why he or she is ending the relationship. He or she might discuss the changes in the relationship both sides have gone through and the faults of both people in the relationship. Justifying the breakup is one of the best ways to get the other person to understand the relationship is over. This strategy is employed when the people involved have an intimate, committed relationship. It can also lead to a positive outcome for the breakup. The people involved still feel loss, but now they understand what led to the dissolution of the relationship. Unfortunately, there can be a dark side to the justification strategy. If the person breaking off the relationship focuses on the faults and shortcomings of the other person as the reasons why the relationship failed, a positive end to the relationship is unlikely to happen. The other person will get his or her feelings hurt and likely have a lowered self-esteem.

DATES WITH OTHER PEOPLE

"I just need a break from you. I'm going on a date this weekend, and I think you should find someone else to date, too. I just need to see what else is out there. I'm not sure where we stand with each other right now."

The **dates with other people** breakup strategy is less clear on the status of the relationship after the announcement. The person who initiates this strategy says he or she would like to start dating other people and encourages his or her partner to start dating other people, too. The other party is not likely to understand this strategy. It also imposes the will of the person breaking up on his or her partner without the partner having any input in the matter. The bright side of this strategy is that the person initiating the breakup is interested in taking a break from a relationship, particularly if it is intimate and intense. In this case, the relationship can eventually start up again. However, this is used to break up permanently.

DE-ESCALATION

"Things just aren't going that well. So let's take a break from each other. We can still be friends. We can still have lunch together, but shouldn't we see if we might be happier apart? If we still have feelings for each other at the end of three months, we can get back together, alright?"

A related strategy is **de-escalation**. In this strategy, the person wanting to break up suggests that the relationship takes a step back. As opposed to pseudo de-escalation, actual de-escalation comes clean about the fact that this is a breakup of sorts, even as the person talking about de-escalation talks about seeing if the relationship can survive the split. This still leaves the possibility of reconciliation in the other person's mind, although rarely does the reconciliation ever take place. An example of de-escalation is the trial separation married couples go through before getting divorced.

THREATS AND BULLYING

"I don't know why I dated you. You are so spineless. I am breaking up with you, and you better go along with it. I still have those pictures of you. Would you like to see them posted on the Internet? Do you think our friends will still look at you the same way? While we are at it, if I hear you tell anyone I was mean to you, I can print those pictures and send them to your parents."

Threats and bullying is a less positive strategy, with a name that says exactly what the person who wants the breakup does to his or her partner. Although this might include threats of what the person will do to the other if he or she refuses to accept the breakup, it also includes threatening his or her partner about his or her behavior after the relationship — for instance, promising revenge on the partner if he or she divulges any embarrassing information about him or her. This is a destructive type of breakup. It wrecks any chance of a friendship afterward and makes the partner feel powerless, which is likely, given the usual loss of self-esteem at the end of a relationship. Another possibility is that the partner might counter the initial threats with threats of his or her own, leading to other negative outcomes.

RELATIONSHIP TRICK TALK

"We just don't agree on anything anymore. You like to watch TV marathons, and I like to exercise. We argue all the time about where to eat, what to eat, and even whose turn it is to clean out the litter box. I want to solve these problems, but now that I've said all that, it seems like the best thing to do might just be to break up."

The **relationship trick talk** is related to the justification strategy, only less direct. It starts with the partner who wants to break up telling his or her partner he or she would like to discuss problems in the relationship and solve them. However, this talk leads the person doing the breaking up to the conclusion that the relationship's problems are unsolvable and the only strategy is to break up. Because the talk is initiated by the person wanting the breakup, he or she has control of the conversation and can structure it to steer his or her partner toward the conclusion that the only possible solution is to break up. If this strategy goes well, both people in the relationship walk away feeling that they tried to save the relationship, even though breaking up was the best thing to do. If it does not go well, the partner can feel betrayed or manipulated. According to Baxter's research, 27 percent of the breakups observed in the study involved a partner using the relationship trick talk.

POSITIVE TONE

"We had fun. The problem is that we want different things out of life. You're a wonderful woman, and I don't think you will have any problem with finding a guy who is everything you want. It's just not me."

One unilateral direct breakup strategy, the **positive tone** method, is designed to make the person who is being dumped feel better about the relationship. Although one of the common lines used in this strategy is, "It's not you, it's me," the positive tone strategy can also encompass the person breaking up telling his or her partner he or she loved the relationship while it lasted, that he or she will find someone else who loves him or her, or that he or she has other priorities that would make a relationship with him or her impossible to sustain. Although this strategy is a direct one, the person being dumped might still interpret the positive tone to mean the relationship could be rekindled or resurfaced at a later date. A person who uses this strategy needs to be clear the breakup is permanent to be successful.

WHAT IS THE BEST WAY TO BREAK UP?

During this discussion of breakup strategies, you might find yourself wondering if there is an ideal way to break up with someone. Strategies, such as the indirect ones, are almost guaranteed to hurt your partner unless both of you want to end the relationship and do not want to be direct about it. Direct is better, although even the justification and positive tone strategies have their downsides. The best advice is to treat your ex the way you would want to be treated. Have the courtesy to break up with your partner the same way.

After reading this, you will have a better idea of how your relationship ended. Even if you were the one who initiated the breakup, you have a better sense of what happened between you and your ex. Simply understanding the process does not make the outcome any easier, though. The question is, how do you deal with the grief you carry?

Chapter 2

Coping With Grief

After suffering from a significant loss, the natural reaction is to feel grief that can rival levels people feel when someone close to them has died. This is understandable and is expected. According to current psychological studies, people who are diagnosed with a terminal illness or who suffer a catastrophic loss go through five stages of grieving. Since psychiatrist Elisabeth Kübler-Ross first introduced this concept in 1969, the five stages are properly known as the **Kübler-Ross model**. People do not have to be dying or be close to someone to experience these stages. Getting your heart broken is loss enough.

Denial

The first stage of the Kübler-Ross model is **denial**, also known as "not just that river in Egypt." This stage is refusing to accept the relationship is over. It is easier to deny the relationship is finished if your ex has not been direct about breaking up with you. For instance, if he or she wants to date other people, you can easily convince yourself he or she just wants a change of pace and will come back to you. If he or she wants to de-escalate the relationship, you can convince yourself he or she just needs his or her space. However, people have been known to still be in denial about an ex who is plainly stating his or her desire to break up.

Denial comes in three flavors. The first is called **simple denial**, which is straightforwardly denying that something exists or has happened. "He didn't break up with me. He just said he was going to date other people." This is the most straightforward means of denial, but it is also hard for someone to convince himself or herself that something simply did not happen. This method of denial is commonly used when someone is confronted with a serious trauma, such as rape or a terminal illness.

Another common means of denial is **minimization**. This stage admits, "Something happened, but it cannot be as serious as it appears." Someone in this type of denial might think, "He said he was breaking up with me, but he didn't mean it. He's just showing me how serious he is about me being late to pick him up."

Then there is the state of denial known as **projections**. At this stage, you admit the facts and their seriousness, but instead of accepting responsibility, you project it onto someone else — in this case, your ex. This is rarely used when trying to deny that a breakup has happened, although it might be used when thinking about who was responsible for the breakup.

Eventually, though, the denial stage ends. It has to end because continuing to deny it flies in the face of reality. Although a person might be able to live in denial about some things, such as the reason he got fired from a job or that he is overweight, living in denial about something such as a breakup will only last until his former love starts dating other people or gets engaged — or even married. Then he will have to face reality because he does so on his own or because his denial of the facts leads to a confrontation, such as his ex filing a complaint against him and getting a restraining order. Unfortunately, facing the situation as it is requires delving into the following stages, which are in the negative end of the emotional spectrum.

Anger

The next stage of the Kübler-Ross model is **anger**. The anger that people feel at the end of a relationship is the kind of anger that arises when someone feels deliberately treated unfairly or harmed by someone else. Someone in this stage will be constantly asking why this loss is happening to him or her. Conversely, he or she will also start to question why other people are not feeling this kind of loss, or if they are, why it is not affecting them as much. This leads to him or her being consumed with anger and envy. This means that the anger one feels at losing a relationship is projected to others, instead of being directed at himself or herself or at his or her ex.

When someone is angry, he or she might express it one of two ways: passively or aggressively. **Aggressive anger** entails the results you would expect, from threatening others — verbally or nonverbally — and bullying other people up to and including physical violence. Aggressive anger can also be expressed by wanting to destroy something, whether it is an object, such as a dish or an urge to harm someone else. The destructive urge might be expressed by destroying other things, such as a relationship between two people or a friendship between the angry person and an acquaintance. People who express their anger aggressively might also be overtly selfish.

However, someone might also aggressively express their anger by being manic and grandiose, as though they possess more energy than they know how to handle. They might go on a spending spree or channel their anger into a marathon exercise session or long workday.

Passive anger, on the other hand, is not expressed as directly as aggressive anger. You might know it by its other name — passive aggression. It can manifest itself as the person performs saint-like acts of self-sacrifice, acting as though he or she is suffering and eating up the gratefulness he or she receives for his or her actions or refusing help entirely, preferring to be seen as a martyr. He or she might also berate themselves in public, apologizing for things that are not even his or her fault, and all but openly invite people to criticize him or her, inviting people to martyr him or her in front of others. People who display their anger passively might also become evasive, avoiding conflict and backing down from crises. They might even exhibit a phobia of conflict.

Less publicly, passive anger can display itself as being obsessive, by making sure things are done perfectly, and trying to apply standards of perfection to activities better done in moderation, such as dieting or exercising. The effects of passive anger might also express themselves as ineffectualness, where the person with anger issues sets themselves up for failure through mechanisms — ignoring serious issues while focusing on insignificant issues, relying on people who are not reliable, or being prone to having accidents. Perhaps the ultimate expression of passive anger is where it becomes dispassionate, as the person abandons all feeling and spends more time with objects or intellectual hobbies instead of interacting with people. When someone who is dispassionate with anger has to interact with others, his or her emotions are insincere. He or she tends to not respond to other people's emotions well and lets other people take charge of problems while he or she sits on the sidelines.

Passive anger is as destructive as aggressive anger. Psychological manipulation is one example, when a person provokes other people to be aggressive and then feigns innocence. He or she might undercut people, subtly insult them — "That dress makes you look less fat than that dress you wore yesterday" — or talk behind other people's backs, gossiping or submitting anonymous complaints to teachers or supervisors. In extreme cases, this type of manipulation can even entail stealing from others and trying to defraud them.

After reading these ways to express anger, you might be feeling as though someone who feels angry is an absolute monster waiting to be unleashed on an unsuspecting world. The truth is that everyone feels angry, and breakups are a time when feelings of anger surface. Also, few people use these ways to express their anger, whether it is aggressive or passive.

In a breakup, the person who has been dumped is likely going to be furious with his or her ex, and his or her anger might expand to include other people, such as the ex's family and friends. He or she might also take his or her anger out on friends, family, and acquaintances. It is during this time that the person going through anger is left to rage at the world and everyone in it on his or her own. People offering help or comfort at this stage might find themselves the target of insults or accusations — things the person will regret when he or she has calmed down.

TALES OF REVENGE

The popular urban legends told on the Internet have to do with people getting revenge on their exes or ways a person ended a relationship. There is the woman who sold her ex-husband's sports car for $100 because her husband wanted her to sell it and give him half the money, the ex-husband who filled the car of his wife's lover with concrete, and the ex-girlfriend who made a long-distance call from the ex-boyfriend's phone while he was on vacation, then left it off the hook. However, there is one tale of revenge that is true. In Sonnenberg, Germany, a mason going through a divorce chain-sawed his single-story house in two, giving half of it to his ex-wife. The law was unhappy with his unique methods and punished him for the stunt. So while people consider and even go through with masterful revenge strategies, you are better off leaving the fantasies in your imagination.

Bargaining

"Maybe if I get my master's degree, he'll fall in love with me again."

"If she comes back to me, I'll stop hanging out with my friends three nights a week."

"If I made more money, would that change the way you feel about me?"

Welcome to the next stage of grieving. It is the sense that you can put off the inevitable or change it entirely — if only you could figure out what that one thing is that will make your ex change his or her mind. This is known as the **bargaining** stage, and as you stop being angry, you start to ask what you can do to make the other person take you back. In the traditional stages of grief, bargaining is talking to God or fate itself, to ask to live long enough to see a particular event happen, ranging from seeing someone's graduation ceremony to living two months longer than expected. This represents a step forward, psychologically speaking. When someone reaches this stage while going through a breakup, psychologically he or she has accepted the relationship is over, even if he or she is trying to delay the breakup.

Bargaining with another person is different from bargaining with death. When trying to bargain in a relationship, you might hit on the right thing to say or do what will make the other person reconsider. Unlike bargaining with death, the other person is capable of changing his or her mind; maybe, you think, if you change the right thing about yourself, your ex will take you back. It does not hurt your chances that the person who broke up with you is feeling remorse of his or her own. However, one change will not put your relationship back together, or the breakup is only put off, not averted.

Depression

"I have lost her; I have lost everything. What is the point of life?"

"Why bother going to work or doing the laundry? It will not bring him back."

"What is the use? It does not works out."

After the fighting has been done and the bargains have been made, **depression** sets in. This is where the feelings of grief are finally processed and, unfortunately, it is not pretty. During bouts of depression, feelings of hopelessness, sadness, and helplessness mix together. The person going through this stage might become withdrawn and introspective and spend time crying and mourning the loss of the relationship.

People coping with depression also do not feel like doing anything, which is why one of the common images of someone who has just gone through a breakup is the person on the couch, ice cream or video game controller in hand, watching the television for days.

How deeply people sink into depression after a breakup depends on several factors, including the length of the relationship, the depth of the relationship, and the amount of time spent together. Fortunately, this stage passes. Psychologists refer to this as slight depression, and the cure is time, getting some sleep, and support from family and friends. However, severe or clinical depression might occur as a result, and this can require psychiatric treatment. One in six adults suffers from depression, and while breaking up will not necessarily lead to severe depression, as a stressful event, it is a significant risk factor.

BROKEN HEART SYNDROME

Can you die of a broken heart? Believe it or not, there is such a thing as "broken heart syndrome."

Broken heart syndrome is referred to as stress cardiomyopathy. It is brought on by extreme and sudden emotional trauma. Although this can include undergoing a breakup, it is brought on by something more severe, such as experiencing the unexpected death of a loved one, being robbed at gunpoint, or being abused by a boyfriend or girlfriend. There are even some reports of broken heart syndrome being brought on by a surprise party.

The sufferers of this issue are women, ones who are postmenopausal. The symptoms are similar to having a heart attack, and although heart failure is the same result for broken heart syndrome and a heart attack, they are not the same. Scientists have found that sufferers of broken heart syndrome have an odd type of weakness on the apex of the left ventricle of the heart. Although this might be an indicator of risk for the syndrome, there is no way to know for sure. Fortunately, if the sufferer can get to a hospital and receive care in time, he or she will survive and the weakness on the left ventricle will disappear. Experts theorize that broken heart syndrome is an unusual response to the chemicals the body generates during and after emotional trauma, such as adrenaline.

Acceptance

The final stage of grief is **acceptance**, when the grieving person realizes the loss has taken place, and he or she is at peace with the loss. He or she realizes that things will get better and that the loss, while painful, will not define him or her.

In the acceptance stage, a person will begin to live his or her life again. In terms of relationships, this means he or she might start dating again, or at least might be open to the possibility. He or she will also start to take responsibility and begin handling day-to-day tasks that he or she had ignored before while in the previous stages of grief. This is the most positive stage of the grieving process because it signifies the person is ready to move on with his or her life.

Acceptance should not be confused with a similar feeling — **resignation**. While actual acceptance entails understanding of the loss and being at peace with it, resignation is being submissive to the loss, even while harboring negative feelings. It is being constantly frustrated at the situation, even while being aware you cannot change it, so why bother trying? This might lead to similar surface results as acceptance. The person appears calm, after all, and he or she is going about his or her normal routine as though nothing were wrong. After time has passed, though, friends and family might notice he or she does not put as much effort into living as he or she once did, or that he or she is more pessimistic than he or she was before the breakup. Acceptance is facing the situation as it is. Resignation is giving in.

Moving Through the Stages

At this point, you might be reading over the stages of grief and thinking, "I didn't deny anything. I just got depressed, then got angry, then got depressed again — what gives?"

No one reacts the same way to grief; Kübler-Ross mentioned that no one experiences the stages of grief in the same order, and people grieving will not experience every step of the model. However, a grieving person will experience at least two of the stages. More commonly, a person will hop from stage to stage and return to various stages multiple times before working through them. The important thing is that you will work through the process — at your own pace.

HOW TO BREAK UP IF A RELATIONSHIP TURNS VIOLENT

Get out. Period. If a relationship turns violent, the problem is not the lack of communication or the failure to address issues in the relationship. It is about not letting yourself be hurt. Although you might think you can work with your partner through this, the odds of a relationship becoming non-violent again with no outside help are low. Repeat domestic abuse in an abusive relationship is so common that it has its own cycle. It starts with the abuser harming the victim then feeling guilt over his or her actions. He or she then asks the victim to forgive him or her. If the victim grants it, the couple has a "honeymoon" period of reconciliation. The honeymoon lasts until the abuser becomes stressed again. After his or her stress level has built up enough, he or she takes it out on his or her partner by abusing him or her, which begins the cycle anew. Do not assume that just because the abuser feels guilty about his or her actions, the relationship will get better.

According to data Erin Marcus gathered in 2008, 10 women a day die from domestic violence in the United States, which totals 3,650 women a year. Every 12 seconds, a woman is beaten by her significant other. Need more incentive to leave an abusive relationship? In 2008,

511,000 women and 105,000 men were victims of domestic violence — enough people to fill a medium-sized city. Once a relationship turns violent, the time for talk is over, and the time for leaving is immediate. No matter what problems a relationship has, abuse is the ultimate deal-breaker. The National Coalition Against Domestic Violence advocates this sentiment, and you can learn more at its website at www.ncadv.org.

How to Cope Through the Stages of Grief

In a serious loss, such as a breakup, denial can manifest itself by your mind refusing to process the information. People report staring at the wall for hours on end as they try to come to grips with the fact that their relationship is over, or come to an understanding that they have suffered a serious loss, but letting their mind slide over what that loss is. This is known as shock, and it might take time for your mind to overcome it.

What is the best way to get over your denial? Acknowledge that your relationship is over. Then acknowledge that you feel hurt because of it. Your mind might want to stop thinking and go back into shock during this process. If it does, give it some time to recover, then acknowledge the loss again. Talking to yourself can do wonders here. Express how you feel, no matter how bad it is. Talk about whether you are angry or depressed, talk about how you feel toward your ex, and get everything out in the open with yourself. Only do this in your own home. If you have roommates, wait until they are gone; this is something you must do for yourself, by yourself.

When confronting your denial, it is important not to fool yourself about the seriousness of the situation. You and your ex are not just going through a bad patch in your relationship; this is not a temporary separation. If you are aware that this breakup is permanent and you cannot bring it back, do not let yourself think otherwise. You will be doing yourself a favor if you just accept the grief instead of putting it off.

Introspection, devastation, and flashes of emotion

After you overcome your disbelief of the situation and accept it, you are ready to face the next stage. This is a hard one to get through because this is where your feelings about the breakup make themselves known. These feelings can seem overpowering, and when you are in their grip, life can seem surreal. You feel disconnected from other people and tasks you are performing. The pain can be so strong that it takes a toll on your body. You feel so consumed with these feelings that getting out of bed takes an effort worthy of an Olympic athlete, and trying to take care of the day-to-day tasks of living now seems insurmountable.

Fortunately, these feelings do not last long. Instead, they come in bursts or spasms. When these bursts of grief hit you, they will not last forever. Narrow your focus down to getting through the rest of the hour, minute, or even second if you need to. Positive self-talk counts in this stage. Keep telling yourself you are going to get through this period, and everything will be better on the other end. This is not idle talk, either. You will feel better when you get through the current burst of grief, and you will feel better after you have passed through the anger and depression.

Review and rumination

During this period, you will also replay your relationship in your head as you are working through your heartbreak. Flashes of good times will be interspersed with the breakup scene, and thoughts of your ex as the person you fell in love with will come to mind. So will thoughts of your ex as he or she is now. It can be extremely frustrating to work with because during this time, you might feel you would be happier forgetting the relationship ever existed.

Despite how you are feeling about them, these flashes of memory are positive steps your mind is taking to process the breakup. Your romantic relationships can play a large role in your life, and relationships are built on memories and information. The only way you can let go of the relationship is for the mind to understand what the relationship was between you and your ex. This is an area where people feel compelled to talk to their ex about the relationship to get closure, but the truth is that you will have to come up with the answers yourself, as your brain reviews the relationship in light of the breakup and comes to understand it and integrate it into your experience.

One of the best ways to cope with this is to keep a journal of what you are thinking and feeling. If one particular area of the relationship seems especially strong, write it in your journal and think about why it resonates so strongly with you. You will hear this advice throughout this book, but writing down the thoughts going through your head codifies them and makes them easier for your mind to understand. The more your mind can understand what is going on, the easier it will be able to process the information and the sooner you will get over your heartbreak.

Coping with anger

When you lose something you cherish, feeling angry is as natural as feeling depressed. This does not mean to act on your feelings. There are ways anger can manifest itself, none of which have a positive outcome. However, even though acting out your anger is bad, that does not mean not to confront it. Repressed anger comes through in other ways and makes a person mean-spirited and bitter. People who have repressed their anger might be constantly annoyed or prone to something putting them in a bad mood. When they interact with people, they might snipe at them, delivering little below-the-radar insults that leave people feeling bad, even if they have no solid evidence that they were insulted.

To deal with your anger, the first thing you need to do is confront it. This anger is yours. Everything you are feeling as a result of this anger belongs to you. Acknowledging this might not be your proudest moment, but once you do, you can start to manage it. When you are aware you are angry, you can also understand who you are angry at, which is not the person in front of you who is not driving fast enough, the group of teenagers laughing and playing in the park, or the old lady in the express checkout lane with 64 cans of vegetables who is counting out the exact amount of change in pennies. Know whom you are getting angry at and why you are getting angry with them.

When you confront your anger, you might feel it is overwhelming you. You have energy, and you might want to take it out on someone. There are positive ways to channel that energy.

- Take any correspondence between you and your ex and rip it up. You might have to print out some of your ex's e-mail to rip them up, but it will feel satisfying when you do it.

- Make a punching bag or buy one from a sporting goods store. Hit it as hard as you can for as long as you can. A pillow is an acceptable substitute for a punching bag.

- Hit the gym or go swimming. Turn that energy into a trim, fit body.

- Talk with an understanding friend about how angry you are.

- Put on some music and sing along. Heavy metal bands work particularly well.

- Meditate. Take deep breaths and try to calm down.

If you feel that you might lose control when you express your anger, or if you feel that when you get angry you cannot hold it in, you might want to see an anger therapist. A place to start your search is at **www.4angertherapy.com.**

Dealing with depression

When you confront and manage your anger, you will find sadness on the other side. People in anger therapy, after having exhausted their rage supply, find that they start crying. One theory is that anger and sadness have the same core negative feeling. When it is turned on oneself, the result is depression. When it is turned on the rest of the world, it becomes anger.

Feeling depressed over the demise of a relationship is as natural as feeling anger. Human beings want to be loved, and when their feelings of love are rejected, they normally will feel depressed. If this is your first experience with heartbreak, you might feel alarmed at how intense your sadness can become. When you feel constantly tired or if you discover you cannot concentrate after a breakup, it is due to being depressed. Although feeling angry can give you excess energy, depression saps it from you. Feeling listless is common. So is feeling weak, which is alright because you might not have the motivation to do anything.

These periods of depression will pass. Although you are in the grip of them, though, you can do things to lessen your pain. Take out your journal again and write down why you are feeling depressed. This will help organize your thoughts in the same way it does during the times when your mind starts ruminating about your relationship and help you to understand your thoughts so you can work through them. Talking with friends is also a way to get through depression.

When you are coping with depression, surrounding yourself with positive thoughts can help. Focus on positive moments that happened during the day or during the week. Think about what you have accomplished, regardless of how small it is. You accomplished it in spite of being depressed. If there are any songs that make you feel better, give them a listen.

People can experience deep depression as a result of the breakup, or they become suicidal. This is not normal, and if you experience this, get help as soon as possible. Although you are aware of what feeling suicidal means, you might be less sure about the symptoms of deep depression. Feeling clinically depressed entails being so depressed you cannot function, and that there is no hope things will get better.

If you have not experienced this before, you might be puzzled about how you can tell whether you have hope, so here is a simple test. Look at yourself in the mirror and ask, "Are things going to get any better?" If you still have hope, you will be able to answer yes, no matter how much you qualify it. Even an answer like, "Things have to eventually get better" counts as a yes. If you do not have hope, on the other hand, even if you can bring yourself to say, "Yes," you will know you are lying. This is not an official psychological test, but it can be an indicator that you might want to visit a therapist.

If you feel suicidal, or if you feel that you are depressed beyond your capacity to function, go to an emergency room. If you feel that even contacting an emergency room is beyond your capacity, contact a friend and have him or her get you there. Emergency rooms are equipped to handle psychological emergencies, and they will be able to provide you with some immediate care and summon a therapist to determine the best course of action.

People refuse to get treatment for mental health issues, even if they suspect they might need it because going to a psychologist is incorrectly perceived as a sign of weakness. While getting psychological help might not initially sound as noble or heroic as facing your problems yourself, the reality is that getting help when you need it is smart, not weak, and admitting you have a problem and facing up to reality takes more courage than being in denial about the situation and waiting to be overwhelmed by reality. As movie director John Carpenter once said, "A strong man likes the feel of nature on his back, but a smart man knows when to get in out of the rain."

CASE STUDY: GETTING THROUGH THE GRIEF

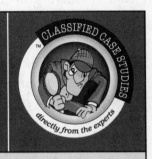

Kara L.C. Jones had a different experience with heartbreak but experienced the same sense of grief and loss that one would in a breakup. She discusses how her journey through the grieving process has helped her to counsel others going through the same stages.

My own heartbreak came, not from a breakup, but from the death of my son on March 11, 1999. He died at birth after a full-term, perfectly healthy pregnancy. So to hear, "Your baby has no heartbeat," instead of, "It's a boy," was heartbreaking to say the least. In that first week after his death, the grief was too overwhelming to do much more than just feel miserable. Well-meaning friends and family were telling us things like, "You're young. You can try again." But the abyss between what I had wanted and what I now faced was just too big to be comforted by any such clichés. I found that creativity was my one safe haven. Making art was part of it, but it was also an everyday creativity. After all, it took creativity to find reasons why I should even bother getting out of bed each day after his death.

As time progressed and I had more energy, I got more adventurous in my creative explorations. Creative tools worked for me, such as art-making, writing in form, and guided visualization. Later, I began sharing my experiments with others in what became my Grief & Creativity Coaching practice. I found the techniques that worked for me as I had moved through the heartbreak of our son's death were the same techniques that worked for clients dealing with relationship breakups.

In particular, there are ideas clients have said were helpful to them during breakups:

1) **Facing the abyss between what was wanted and what is now.** We do guided visualizations together to see and feel ourselves standing at the edge of what we had wanted. We allow ourselves to face this abyss of loss and look for the bridges that might let us cross to a more peaceful space, remembering our broken hearts. Some clients find it helpful to journal or do collage work afterward to explore the visualizations.

2) Practicing permission. We look at where we are stopping ourselves. We ask ourselves honestly where we are not granting ourselves permission. And then we create permission slips for ourselves to allow for practicing how to do and feel whatever we need to do and feel. Examples: "I have permission to just be in my funk and see what is there," "I have permission to grieve in more than five stages," or "I have permission to celebrate the holiday and feel icky at the same time."

It allows us to make visible what might otherwise be invisible, tucked away inside, as we put on our masks to try and get back to work or do the things demanded of us in our everyday lives.

3) Letting our experiences transform to get a different perspective. For this one, you pick some element of nature that represents your experience, such as a storm. Then you list all the attributes of a storm: windy, dark, cold, unpredictable, and damaging. And then you journal about your experience using those attributes — the idea being that you get a look at your experience in a different light or as something more outside yourself. An example using "gale-force winds" as the element:

Gale Force, by Kara L.C. Jones

I used to be a gale, soaring into any room with an outburst of laughter, a pouring of sunny miracles. But since my son died, I am a sallow fog, a damp veil hanging from thin air with the ability to unsettle the marrow from your bones. Birds don't like my moist tears on their wings, but some — like the black birds — gather to crow dirges, giving voice to sorrow over the lands. I used to be a gale who would just breeze by. Now I am a mist, a permanent part of your land.

Some clients like to write in journal style, while others might write in poetic format. Other clients like to take the element of nature they choose and cut out images from old magazines that illustrate the attributes. Then they will make collage art exploring the "storm of grief" or whatever they are experiencing in the moment.

None of this is about finding *the answers*. It is about showing up consciously for whatever you are feeling and allowing those feelings to be expressed. It is about expressing your experience in a different way so that you might glimpse a different perspective and shift your process. Each small expression experiment helped me in some way to begin understanding an otherwise overwhelming heartbreak. Creativity, in forms and formats, was my heartbreak salve.

Anxiety and guilt

Two close cousins of depression are anxiety and guilt. Neither is pleasant.

When anxiety hits, such as when you see your ex unexpectedly, you might mistake it for restlessness, at least until it increases. When it becomes worse, anxiety feels as though your body is on red alert against an unknown threat. Your hands might shake, your heart might feel like it has gotten a dose of adrenaline, and you will notice every movement and noise. At higher levels, anxiety can cause you to lose sleep or be unable to eat. Although these problems can be solved with medication, you might want to practice some techniques to help you relax.

Pick a room, such as your den or bedroom, to serve as your relaxation room. Buy some candles for it, and make sure you can adjust the blinds to make the lighting more subdued. Get some calming music, or buy a CD full of white noise, such as rainstorm or beach sounds. Then lie down and try to picture yourself somewhere, which is easier if you have one of the white noise CDs. Lie there until you feel calm again, and repeat this technique. You might also want to add some of your own touches to this room, such as scented candles or incense because this technique is similar to meditation. The more relaxed you become, the less anxiety will affect you.

Guilt, on the other hand, has no physical symptoms. In relationships, both sides will feel guilty it ended. If you broke up with your partner, you might feel guilty that you did not try harder to save the relationship. If you have been broken up with, you might feel guilty that you did not do enough in the relationship to make your partner happy with it. At this point, you might feel you can come up with a dozen things you could have done better in your relationship without having to think hard.

What is especially insidious about guilt is that it leads you to think you still have some control over the breakup. Because the dissolution of the relationship was your fault, that must mean you can apologize and make things better again, right?

But the problem is that even if you apologize, you cannot change the past. If you did not commit one of the unforgivable sins of a relationship, such as cheating on or abusing your partner, then you did not do any one thing to cause the relationship to fail. Even if you can come up with some definite ways you were a bad boyfriend or girlfriend, you cannot beat yourself up over them. It is unproductive at best and, at worst, the guilt will prevent you from being in another romantic relationship for a long time, until you learn to forgive yourself. While you cannot move on if you believe you can apologize enough, you also cannot move on as long as you keep beating yourself up.

If you want to impress your ex, take responsibility for the mistakes you made, then put those lessons to use in your next relationship. If you and your ex ever meet again, he or she will be impressed with how you have changed. Take out your journal and write about your guilty feelings in there. Discuss how you can put those lessons to use in your next relationship. If you still feel guilty, you can write a letter of apology to your ex. Write down everything you would like to say to him or her, then seal it in an envelope or save it to your computer. Avoid mailing it until after you are over your ex.

None of the above

At some point, all these intense emotions you have been feeling will collide and, in the grand tradition of equal and opposite forces everywhere, cancel each other out and leave you in a state of **ambivalence**, or uncertainty about how to feel. You might feel calm, somewhat at peace, and perhaps even indifferent to your breakup during this state. Although this might be a relief, as you are now free from these intense negative emotions that have been threatening to consume you, feeling ambivalent can also be confusing. The sensation of feeling nothing when you feel you should be feeling something can be disconcerting, and you might wonder what is wrong with you.

Unlike other emotional states during the grieving process, this is one for which to feel thankful. Appreciate the calmness your mind is giving you, and take this moment to relax. The other feelings will be back, and you will continue on the grieving process.

Allow yourself the time to feel other emotions, then work with the anger and sadness.

Accepting and moving on

The final stage, **acceptance**, is something to welcome, not cope with. You might not realize you are in the acceptance stage until after the fact, such as when you drive to work and realize you have not thought about your ex for a week. Acceptance begins with brief periods of being at peace with yourself among the feelings of depression and anger. In time, these periods grow longer, and the periods of depression and anger become shorter.

The acceptance period brings with it a new understanding of what life is about. There might not be just one right answer to what life is about, but at this point, you have found the answer that works for you. This newfound clarity results in people going through their life and reevaluating it — a spiritual spring cleaning. During this time, people might make major changes based on their newfound clarity. They might decide to become serious about things they have dreamed of doing, they might decide to move to a new city in a new state, or they might go back to school or go into a new career.

When you are in the middle of this phase, enjoy it. You have earned the right after what you have been through in the wake of the breakup. Consider the goals you want to achieve with your new understanding, and use the courage and strength you have acquired as a result of this process to their best advantage.

Now it is time to start discussing areas of the breakup in depth. What is the best way to cope with seeing your ex again? What do you do for fun now that your ex is not around? Where do you go from here? The answers are just ahead.

```
CASE STUDY:
MOVING THROUGH
THE GRIEVING PROCESS
```

Faydra Rector is a certified life coach with an Master of Arts in psychology and more than 14 years of experience in the field of relationships. She writes a weekly newspaper column called "Life Coach" for the Red Bluff Daily News and is starting up a one-hour radio show under the same topic.

Here is her advice on coping with breakups, particularly when there are children involved.

The biggest problem I see people trying to overcome is allowing themselves to go through the cycle of grief, as shown by this chart:

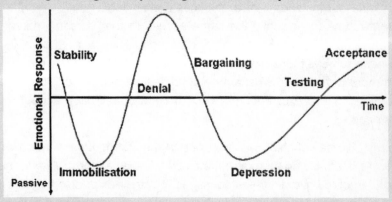

Any loss falls into the grief cycle. A breakup is no different. My clients get stuck in one phase of grief and sit there for years. For example, there are people who become so angry at their ex or the circumstances that surround the breakup that they take that anger with them into any new relationship. They, in essence, could not make their partner pay, so they transfer that "balance due" to everyone else. Once I help them see they have taken this baggage with them, they are horrified to see what they have done.

Another way that they stay stuck is by refusing to accept or let go of the situation. People tend to romanticize their relationships when they are over-analyzing the issues that led to the breakup. This can keep them in the denial or bargaining phase of the grief cycle. I try to help people see that there are legitimate issues when a relationship does not work out. The sooner people acknowledge that they need to say goodbye to the "dream" they had, the sooner they can heal and find the life they desire.

The depression phase of the relationship grief cycle can stymie people from making personal choices that will move them closer to healing. People eat too much or too little, exercise too much, or let it all go. The sense of the relationship being all they will ever have becomes a bigger loss issue than the hope of finding a new and better life. Age and economics also play a huge role in this.

In the case of marriage or children involved, there will likely be an ongoing relationship. I work with clients to stay real about the shortcomings of the individual and to understand their relationship is no longer based on love, but instead, is of a business relationship. I coach people to realize they do not have the same access to that person's personal business any longer. That is hard for people. They want to be able to connect in ways that are no longer appropriate. I tell them that they have no more right to know certain personal issues and to contribute their opinions to their exes than they do to the mailman. That is a tough one for people.

In my divorce-coaching practice, one of the first things I work on with people is educating them about their own issues as they relate to their exes. People have deep-seated issues with their ex or else they would not be getting separated. I coach people to realize that they can only control three things in their life: their thoughts, feelings, and actions. They cannot control another person in any way. They might be able to manipulate them, push their buttons, or make them have a hard time, but they cannot control them. Likewise, their exes can push their buttons, make life hard, and do mean things, but they cannot control their responses. People train one another how to treat them. Eleanor Roosevelt said, "No one can make you feel inferior without your consent." Every situation in life simply is until you attach a response to it.

When it comes to having children, I tell my clients that they have to keep their eye on the bigger prize. People want immediate gratification. They want a cause and effect situation when dealings with their exes. For example, if Daddy is mean to Mommy, Mommy wants the children to love her more (consciously or subconsciously); or if Daddy doesn't pay child support, Mommy doesn't want Daddy to have access to the children. The problem with this line of thinking is that the reason Mommy feels slighted is that she thinks the situations are unfair, and our society is taught that justice is best served cold and immediate.

I teach clients that the best thing that they can do in all situations is to operate under three principles: legal, logical, and ethical. Based on that criteria, they should make a non-reactionary decision to their exes when they are mean. Operate in the best interest of the children and your integrity. When you do, it all works out in the end. What parents find is that as their children grow, they begin to realize the drama on their own and formulate their own opinions. As young adults, these children make their own decisions about who operated fairly. The delayed gratification is worth waiting for.

When speaking about your ex, limit your comments to the old adage: If you can't say something nice, don't say anything. Children are not counselors or friends. It is not their role to be your sounding boards or referees. I have had my own issues with my ex, who likes to talk to me through our child. I have learned that he does not want to have direct communication. When he starts a conversation through her, I take the higher road. For example, she comes home and says, "Dad wants to know X, Y, and Z." Instead of further involving her, I take the information and go from there. I follow up with an e-mail, a phone message, or what have you and get her out of the equation as soon as possible. I tell him — when the time is right and under the right circumstances — that I feel it is better to talk to me directly about adult issues.

Also, when children hear their parents speak poorly about their mother or father, it makes them feel they are a part of the problem. It is not lost on them that the only reason you are still involved with their mom or dad is because you have the child in common. Children can become down on themselves if they feel responsible for your pain. Don't allow them to mess up their own value by expressing your distaste for their other parent.

soon as possible. I also tell him — when the time is right and under the right circumstances — that I feel it is better to talk to me directly about adult issues.

Also, when children hear their parents speak poorly about their mom or dad, it makes them feel as though they are part of the problem. It is not lost on them that the only reason you are still involved with their mom or dad is because you have them, the child, in common. Children can become down on themselves if they feel responsible for your pain. Don't allow them to mess up their own value by expressing your distaste for their other parent.

Sometimes the issues that surrounded your breakup can be likened to an addiction. If you are newly sober, you are not going to hang out in a bar. If you are trying to stop being a cheater, you should not go to the strip club. The same is true with your relationship. If you always went to the same place for dinner on Saturday night and sat in the corner booth and drank a mojito, do not go to that place, *ever*.

Do not look at old pictures and romanticize the situation. Likewise, do not look at old pictures and seethe about what a jerk they were. Put the albums away and get rid of the things that make you stay stuck in the grief cycle.

Additionally, train yourself to speak in the present. Your friends want to support you and love your through your mess; make sure you don't spend your time with them talking incessantly about your ex, your drama, and your pain. What you think about and speak about is what you bring about. If all you do is talk about your pain, you leave little room for a new life to seep in.

Chapter 3

The Disengagement Protocols

Now that you have an understanding of how relationships fall apart and what the grieving process is like, you are ready to take on your broken heart. So, what is the first step on the road to recovery? It is simple — do not call.

Although you were with your former partner, you developed some close ties, especially if you were together for years or if you were married. Now that your relationship has ended, you desperately need to talk to someone — someone who knows you, someone who understands you, and someone whom you can count on to make you feel better. Unfortunately, the first person you might think of is your ex. This is the kind of no-win situation that has inspired people to find the nearest convenient wall against which they can pound their heads.

Then again, maybe you do not want your ex to comfort you. Maybe you are doing just fine without him or her, except you just got the car washed and cleaned, and he or she complained about that. What could possibly make him or her happier than calling him or her up and telling him or her that one of his or her biggest pet peeves is no longer a problem? Also, if you call him or her, you can show him or her that you are not the same person you were before. You have changed, and you are the kind of person that he or she wants to spend time with, or maybe even fall in love with. Now, if you could just find the right words to say it.

Do you see the trap? The one person in the world you want to communicate with is the one person with whom you need to cut off all forms of communication. But if you keep talking to your ex, you will not be able to cut the emotional ties with him or her and move on. According to grief counselor Dr. Susan J. Elliott, the one problem common to everyone who struggles through a breakup is that, for whatever reason, they just cannot or do not want to stop communicating with their exes. Even after it is clear the relationship is well and over, people still have trouble shutting off all forms of communication. But if you are ever going to get the space you need to emotionally heal and come to peace with the loss of your relationship, it is a step you must take.

The problem in the 21st century is that being able to communicate with someone is easy. While you can pick up the telephone and easily give your ex a call (you have his or her number on speed dial, right?) or shoot him or her a quick e-mail, you can also check his or her social media sites or contact him or her through instant messaging. He or she can also contact you.

What is the best solution to this problem? You are going to need to steel your resolve. Take a moment and calm yourself. Do whatever you need to do to get yourself in the frame of mind to make a big decision. When you are ready, make a commitment to yourself that you are not going to contact him or her again, in any way, shape, or form. Ideally, do not set any sort of time limit on this communications blackout, but at least maintain it for a month or two.

When you begin your period of no communication with your ex, though, you might want to let him or her know about it, especially if you communicate on a social media site. Write him or her a brief message and say that due to the breakup, you need to spend time away from him or her before you can figure out where the two of you stand. Send it to him or her and then get rid of your ex's contact information. Delete his or her number from your cellphone, go to your e-mail program and delete his or her e-mail address, then unfollow or delete him or her as a friend on any social media pages.

While you can hide your status and updates from your ex, if you do not unfollow him or her, you will be able to see what he or she is doing, unless he or she hides his or her status and updates or unfollows you first. Also, change the relationship status of your social media pages to "single." Do not put this off. The longer you wait to do it, the longer you will be reminded that you were in a relationship with your ex. Setting your social media relationship status to single is like pulling off a bandage quickly. It will hurt at first, but you can start recovering from the pain that much sooner.

Delete him or her from your address book and contact lists, written and digital. If you feel you must keep his or her contact information, write it on an index card. But once you do, put the card out of sight in an area you will not be able to reach easily. Better yet, give the card to a friend and ask him or her to store it in a safe place. Tell him or her not to give it back to you until at least a month has passed.

Once you have that taken care of, the hard part begins. At this point, the void the other person has left is going to make itself known. Whom are you going to talk to now that the person who knew you better than anyone else is gone? What should you do with yourself when the only thing you want to do is call him or her up and just hear him or her say, "Hello?" The good news is that the emptiness created by completely cutting yourself off from your ex eventually disappears. Breaking up with your ex is like overcoming a drug addiction in ways, and to a certain extent, you are psychologically addicted to your ex's company. You need to go through the withdrawal stage to feel better. How long does this take? It depends on the person. People have trouble for a day or two before they realize they are feeling better. Some people might have to wait. Others might have to wait longer.

Fortunately, you will not be alone when you decide to stop having contact with your ex. Contact your family and your friends, and get a sense of times they are available to talk. Let them know you are trying not to talk to your ex, and ask if you could talk to them instead. For your benefit and theirs, make a schedule of when they are available, and make sure you do not rely on one person. When you feel you need to contact your ex, contact one of the people from your list instead.

Throughout the day, make sure you take care of yourself. Falling back into a bad habit is easier if you are physically or mentally exhausted. Get exercise daily to avoid feeling rundown, and if you can, avoid running yourself ragged while at work. Make sure to not skip meals, and get at least eight hours of sleep. Just as important is to do some nice things for yourself. Eat out with friends, or buy that book you have been curious about reading.

That being said, you might still feel the need to contact your ex. If you do, you can take a lesson from people who are going through behavioral therapy for compulsive behaviors, such as overeating — keep a journal. Buy a small notebook, and keep it in easy reach of your computer or phone. The next time you want to contact your ex, or the next time you break down and talk to your ex, get out the journal and write about your state of mind when you called him or her. Write about what you were feeling, what you were thinking, and what you wanted to say. Then, start asking questions. Examine your feelings and ask yourself about why you want to stay in contact. Here are some sample questions to get you started:

- What did I hope to get out of this conversation?

- What do I want to take away from this conversation?

- What do I want my ex to take away from this conversation?

- How do I want to feel after the conversation is done?

- How do I want my ex to feel after the conversation?

- How was I feeling when I decided I wanted to talk to my ex?

- Would you rather receive bad attention from your ex than none?

As you keep track of your emotions, you will be able to realize exactly why you want to contact your ex. After that, you can plan what you will do the next time you feel the urge to call, write, or text. For example, after keeping a journal for a week, you might realize that you get the urge to call your ex after watching the food channel because you liked to cook dinner for your ex, who was appreciative when you did. From there, you can formulate a list of things you can do to stave off the urge. A good plan based on this example is:

CHECKLIST:

♡ First, select a friend who also has an interest in cooking. Talk with him or her and explain how watching the food channel makes you nostalgic for the time you spent with your ex.

♡ Second, go for a walk.

♡ Third, write about how you are feeling. Go back to your journal and pour out your heart to it.

♡ Fourth, go to the gym.

♡ Fifth, cook. Why not let that television episode inspire you? Try out a recipe you have been thinking of, or make an old favorite. Get involved in your hobby and feel happy that you are doing it for yourself. The fact that you can taste the fruits of your labors is an added bonus.

♡ Last, take a shower.

Creating Your Own Plan

"Anyone with a broken heart who enjoys cooking is taken care of, but what about people like me, who like macramé? What about all the rest of us?" The answer is that creating a plan to avoid contact with your ex does not just depend on your hobby. It is a personal process, and you will likely be refining it from day to day.

To start making a plan, get a sheet of paper and read through your journal about all the times you have wanted to call your ex. As you read through your journal, come up with activities that can take your mind off how you feel. Some samples are listed below:

- **Take a shower.** While you might also consider taking a bath, taking a shower is more active because you are washing yourself, washing your hair, and perhaps even shaving while you are standing up. It is more engaging than taking a bath, it will occupy your mind with thoughts other than calling your ex, and as hundreds of movies and romantic novels have shown, it is a way to relieve stress.

- **Exercise.** Burn off extra emotional energy. Plus, exercising raises your serotonin levels, makes you feel better and combats the negative emotions you are feeling.

- **Go for a walk.** Walking is simple activity you can do anywhere, and it will give you time to calm down so your emotions are not in charge anymore.

- **Visit your local mall.** Although buying things is only a temporary fix for unhappiness, activities, such as window-shopping, do not have to include buying anything. This is another activity that will make you feel better and draw attention away from contacting your ex.

- **Visit your neighborhood park.** People like to be in the city, while others enjoy the feel of nature around them. Spending time in your local park is a way to restore your peace of mind, and parks have free-to-use facilities for activities, such as tennis courts, basketball hoops, or disc golf courses.

- **Write in your journal.** The journal does not just have to be for chronicling when you want to call your ex. Pour out your heart to it. Write down everything about how you feel, your state of mind, and try to put into words just why it is that your ex is the only person you need to talk to at this moment. One of the nice things about writing your thoughts down is that you are forced to clarify what you are thinking, and when you are able to go back and read what you have written, you can think about your feelings with a level head.

- **Work on a hobby or craft.** This is another way to regain your peace of mind. Also, hobbies, from doing crossword puzzles to knitting, will give you time to calm down and think about why you want to contact your ex, and why doing so might not be as good an idea as you initially thought. Plus, when you work on a hobby, you are concentrating on your needs, not the needs of your relationship.

- **Do housekeeping.** It might not be as engrossing as you doing a favorite hobby, exercising, or talking to a friend, but if you make a commitment to yourself that you need to clean the dishes or vacuum your bedroom before calling, you will prevent the stereotypical "messy house" syndrome that is a staple of movie and television breakups and will have another way to give yourself a cool-down period, the same way you would as a hobby. Housekeeping is also like a hobby because you are doing something for yourself.

- **Do homework.** This is similar to doing housework because it is less fun than going to the mall, working on a hobby, or talking with a friend. On the other hand, it is something that you need to do anyway, and as you take your mind off your ex, you are doing something for yourself. If you are not in school, you might want to do something similar, such as balancing your checkbook or making sure all the bills have been paid.

Once you come up with a list of activities, pick five or six you think will take your mind off wanting to contact your ex. Make a list, and post it by your telephone. Given that people use their cellphones as their main phone line, a good alternative might be to place your list by your computer to avoid texting your ex. The next time you feel the need to call your ex, go to your list and do the first activity. After you are done with the first activity, if the urge to contact your ex has passed, you can smile and go about your day. If it has not, go to the list again and do the next item. Repeat until you no longer have the urge to contact your ex.

If you end up calling your ex in spite of this list, do not beat yourself up. Go back to your journal and answer the same questions you asked when you came up with your plan. Then think about how the activities you listed did not help you out of your mental state and revise your list accordingly.

Did you just feel you could not help yourself with the telephone and computer in easy reach? Next time, leave your cellphone behind when you go for a walk or visit the mall. Was your hobby the strongest tie you had with your ex? Switch out doing your hobby with another activity. Keep revising this list until you find the activities that work for you. But make sure that they are things you want to do. You might ask other people for their advice on creating this list, but you have the final say in what will heal you. So your friend thinks you should invest some serious money into a bicycle and go out cycling? So your mother says that this is the perfect time to get a membership to the gym and drop those 20 pounds she has been nagging you about for the past year? Figure out if they will help you. If you do not see the appeal in cycling, or you do not want to have to deal with the pressure of trying to lose weight on top of dealing with your breakup, then feel free to discard that suggestion in favor of an activity that works for you.

CASE STUDY: A COUNSELOR WHO HAS BEEN IN THE TRENCHES

If there is one person who should stand as a beacon of light at the end of the breakup tunnel, it should be Ken Donaldson. He has overcome divorce, depression, and addiction to be a psychotherapist, author, speaker, and relationship coach. He is one of six recipients who won the 2006 Tampa Bay Health Care Hero Award, and he is the founder of the Personal Empowerment Coaching Program. Here he shares some advice on getting through your breakup.

"Getting through the pain is the biggest challenge," Ken says, "plain and simple. It feels like it's going to last forever. Or that you're forever scarred. Minutes seem like weeks and days seem like years. And then there's also all the racing thoughts: Trying to figure it all out. 'Why did this happen?' and 'What did I do wrong?' are common, but the [biggest one] is, 'Why does this happen to me?'"

As you work on healing yourself, you need to give yourself time, "as much as you need," according to Ken. "Talk about it with your friends if you need to, and write about it if that helps. But more than anything else, just give it time. Time does heal all wounds, especially if it is guilt-free, shame-free, and resentment-free."

Healing from a broken heart is a different process for everyone, according to Ken. However, he has advice for those going through break-ups. "Use your support system and surround yourself with compassionate and understanding people," he says. "Realize, however, that some people don't know what to do or say, so they do or say things that can be counterproductive. Joining a support group or therapy group can also be beneficial." Ken also cautions against hanging around people who are too zealous in taking your side. "Don't allow the negative people to bombard you with conversation about how bad [your ex] was."

Ken also encourages harnessing your artistic side during the breakup. "Music, dance, and artwork are all forms of self-expression that can be helpful in the healing process," he says.

However, Ken also warns against three behaviors that can impede the healing process. "If you immediately start dating again," he says, "you'll likely carry all the hurt, anger, and whatever else you're feeling right into the next relationship. Also, your thinking and 'picking mechanism' is not going to be grounded and clear during this time, so you're likely to get into something that could be highly dysfunctional."

The second behavior to avoid is playing the blame game. "It's easy to take the other person's inventory and look at everything they did wrong or bad, even if they did do inappropriate things," Ken says. "But what's the point? The more time and energy you spend focused on that, the longer it'll take you to move on."

Finally, do not fall into the mentality of being the victim. "How about this: It's no one's fault. It just happened. Period," Ken suggests. "Even though it might not make sense and even though there might be unanswered questions, this is the time to heal and begin to move forward. Instead of getting into, 'Why does this happen to me?' or 'I can't believe he/she did this to me,' how about, 'Live and let live,' as the people in Alcoholics Anonymous say? Just pay attention to what you need right now. This also includes getting into lengthy discussions with your friends about how bad [your ex] was. It's time to release and mend your own heart. Staying focused on the pain will only keep you focused on the pain."

When the topic shifts to whether to see your ex again, Ken is reluctant to give a hard and fast answer. "It all depends on a number of dynamics," he explains. "If seeing your ex only makes you feel worse, then no. If the two of you fight or argue — maybe just like the old days — then no again. But if the two of you can have a good con-versation, or better yet, a healing conversation, then sure, go ahead and see each other. Can the two of you celebrate the wonderful times you spent together? Can you tell each other what you appreciate about each other? Can you, in a loving way, also share with each other what didn't work or what was unacceptable? Perhaps you can even kindle a friendship from this. Give this all the time it needs, and don't try to rush it. This might be a vulnerable time and you might not be seeing things clearly if there is still emotion going on."

Since everyone heals at an individual rate, there is not a defined time-table for when you feel up to dating again. However, Ken urges people who have suffered a breakup to not rush things. "Better to go slow than fast, as a rule," he says. "People dive into another relationship as a way to avoid the pain from the former one and only make things worse for themselves. When you do start to date again, go slow. Ask questions and remember what you learned from your past relationship. Perhaps your last relationship opened some insights to yourself, things you didn't know about yourself previously. Play those new insights forward and create new boundaries for yourself. Be cautious and keep shuffling your feet forward."

When you finally do go on a date, Ken urges people to be patient. "Re-member what you've learned. Think from your head, not your heart, meaning you need to make sure that you're clear about your deal-mak-ers and deal-breakers and that you stick to your boundaries and limits. If you're not sure about all this, then it's time to get clear. Use your sup-port system to help, or maybe even a counselor if you can't figure this out for yourself."

One of the best traits that can get you through a breakup is decisive-ness, according to Ken. "Decide that [your relationship] is done if it's truly done and begin to heal, recover, and move on. People go back and forth unnecessarily, causing more pain. If you haven't done every-thing possible, then perhaps you'll want to get a counselor involved, but at some point you have to decide to either repair the relationship or move on. Limbo-land will drain the life out of you."

Excuses, Excuses

Another problem that comes up when trying to cut off contact with one's ex is that people can think of reasons why they need to be in touch. There might be something they are looking for their exes to give them, or perhaps they are looking to have that one conversation that will wrap up the relationship so they can continue. Grief counselor Dr. Susan Elliott has found that when someone wants to see his ex again, he will come up with one of seven different reasons why he should contact her. There will be an infinite number of variations on these excuses, but with a little questioning about the person's reasons, one of these excuses will show up.

Closure

The first excuse is getting **closure**, when you have to know what happened to your relationship. If you just knew what went wrong in this relationship, you would be able to close the book on this chapter in your life and move on, free of pain and guilt. The only way you feel you will ever get closure is to talk with your ex and understand how and why this happened.

Getting closure is something people want in their relationships, but thinking it can only be obtained after hashing out your relationship with your ex is a mistake. You might have questions about what went wrong, and these questions might nag at you. However, talking with your ex about these questions does not give you the answers you are looking for. The answers he or she gives you might make sense initially, at least until you start thinking about them. If he or she says, "We could not agree on how to manage money," you might be satiated for a day or so, until you start thinking of the times that you did agree on things to buy or what purchases to avoid, and there will be exceptions to reasons your ex gives. This leads to the conclusion that there must have been a deeper reason, and you need to call your ex again to ask about it. If you happen to be reading this and wincing at the familiarity, do not be too hard on yourself. People have fallen into the trap of thinking that their ex's answers are unsatisfying and that there has to be an even deeper reason.

You also run the risk that the closure you get will make you feel worse. What if your ex sends you one e-mail then refuses to respond to your other questions? What if he or she simply ignores your request for closure entirely? Worse yet, your ex might use this opportunity to excoriate you and list all your faults in alphabetical order or deliver insult after insult about everything relating to you while insinuating that you need to lower your standards from him or her.

Either way, you will have to accept the fact that your ex cannot give you the answers that will give you closure. The closure you seek has to come from within. Also, a large part of that closure will be accepting the fact that life does not give you answers, not even to questions you feel are important. Instead, you need to accept that the experience happened, learn to draw from its lessons, and move on. It is not easy, and there is no one way to do it.

Just one more thing to say

Tied close with the concept of closure is the excuse of saying one last thing. While you might have been questioning your ex about why things went wrong in the relationship, the belief that you need to say one last thing is understandable, especially if you were the one dumped. Again, it is another common cliché in countless love-themed novels and romantic comedies. If you just make one touching display of your love, or say the right thing, your lover will come running back to your arms and not get on that plane to Paris or New Jersey. So, you think to yourself, is there any reason this cannot be your moment?

Unfortunately, there are reasons why this cannot work. The biggest one is that relationships do not just suddenly come into being. Similarly, relationships do not just fall apart overnight. Your relationship might have dissolved when you caught your significant other in bed with someone else, but there was a long, slow road to that point. Either that, or he or she did not intend to be faithful to you. Regardless of the reason, you cannot change your partner's mind over the course of just one conversation. At the least, it would take weeks of talking and convincing to make your partner think the two of you should get back together, and that is only if they are open to the possibility in the first place. Otherwise, you are crossing the fine line from "impassioned" to "stalker," and that can create problems several orders of magnitude above a broken heart. The bottom line is that you two are different people, and as things stand, neither of you are compatible. It is a harsh truth to admit, but the sooner you admit it, the sooner you can start moving on.

Though, the reasoning behind saying one last thing is to prove your ex wrong about his or her view of you. You just need to tell him or her that you are mature, that you are responsible, and that you respect his or her boundaries before you move on with your life. This is similar to closure, but in this instance you need your ex to deny his or her criticisms of you before you can start dating. Given that trying to change his or her mind is going to erupt into an argument before you hang up, he or she is unlikely to take back his or her assessment of you. In terms of an excuse to contact your ex, this is something of a sustaining cycle where you contact him or her, fail to change his or her mind, then contact him or her later, when you are determined to change his or her mind — and he or she is equally determined that you will not.

If you are upset at something your ex said to you during the breakup process, the person whose opinion you need to adjust is yours. Why should his or her opinion of you, especially at a point where negative emotions are running high, matter? Is his or her opinion of you more important than yours? The best thing you can do is repeat, "Who cares what he or she thinks?" If there is one person in this world who should not have to care what your ex thinks, it is you.

MAILING YOUR BREAKUP IN

If you want to contact your ex about something he or she said that hurt you, use the old behavioral therapy method of writing a letter.

The process is simple: When you feel you need to contact your ex about an issue, instead of picking up the telephone or going to your e-mail account, take out a sheet of paper and start writing instead.

Discuss each issue and take as much time as you need to express yourself. Be as emotional as you would like. Then, fold the letter and put it in an envelope. Last, do not send the letter.

Instead, burn it, shred it, or find another way to make sure no one else will read what you have written. This letter is not meant for your ex; it is meant to help you solidify your thoughts about your ex, and writing your thoughts down is an excellent way to express your feelings without running the risk of any hard feelings resulting from sharing them. Writing down your thoughts can also make you aware of the issues you have regarding your ex. And once you know what those issues are, you will have an easier time sorting them out.

If you do not have a pencil or pen and paper, you can turn to the 21st-century equivalent — your computer's word processor. The process is the same, with the exception that you should empty your computer's recycling or garbage bin after deleting the document.

Have to get my stuff back

As far as excuses go, the "returning stuff" reasoning is a thinly disguised excuse to see your ex again. It can also be used to fool yourself. While you might know not to try to get closure or get the last word in, you might realize that your ex still has your favorite sweater, the one you liked so much that you let him or her borrow it. So what choice do you have but to visit him or her — even though you do not want to, and you know that it would be better for all concerned if you did not go there?

If you do want your stuff back from a breakup, you and your ex should agree to do a mutual return within days of the event. The longer you wait, the less justification you will have for trying to get your things back. Also after "a reasonable time" (weeks), your ex can legally assume custody of your stuff and do with it as he or she sees fit. It is a blurry area, legally, but if your ex keeps your stuff, you will be faced with the dilemma of whether to let it go or undergo the cost and time of a trial in small claims court. If you need a good reason to get your stuff back quickly after the breakup, this is it. If you still have things that belong to your ex, or you want some things back from your ex, take time and get all the items you want to return into one pile. Make a list of all the things you want back from your ex. Then contact him or her, make the trade, and do not contact him or her again.

While on the subject of getting stuff back, do not try to get gifts back. They belong to your ex now. One important exception is an engagement ring, which is not a gift. Instead, it is a symbol of commitment given in anticipation of marriage or another indication of a permanent relationship. When the relationship ends, get the engagement ring back as soon as possible, if you were the one who bought it. If you received the engagement ring, you have a responsibility to return it to your ex.

I still want to be friends

As opposed to other excuses, the "let's be friends" reason for keeping in contact might seem like the best way to show you are moving on with your life while still keeping in contact with your ex, making the breakup hurt less. At least, that is the theory. In reality, being friends with your ex after breaking up will drag you into the same pitfalls of contacting your ex that plague those who rely on other excuses. The problem is that you and your ex still need to explore the ruins of your relationship and come to a sense of closure about it. Part of that closure is going to involve getting over your feelings for your ex, and you will not be able to do that if you are still in contact with him or her. You are going to need some time to reestablish yourself as a single person and not part of a couple.

Trying to be friends with your ex is also problematic because of all the history you have with him or her. You can joke around and tease your friends, but with your ex, all the things that make a friendship suddenly become a minefield. Unless you and your ex are formal and polite all the time, the odds are high that one of you will say something that touches on a sore spot in your relationship. It is one thing to tease a friend about how messy his or her room is; it is another to tease your ex about a messy room, especially if that was one of the problems you had with him or her.

Unlike these excuses, though, being friends with your ex after you have broken up is achievable. It just should not be attempted immediately after you have broken up with him or her. Let the bonds between you and your ex dissolve until you start thinking of the two of you as separate entities, as opposed to still being a couple. This is going to take time, and ideally, during that time you will be free of your ex. There is no one-size-fits-all time limit here, but a good rule of thumb is at least a year. People might need more time than that. So at the end of a year, ask yourself honestly if you want to see your ex again to show him or her how much you have grown as a person and how you are now, or if you miss the non-relationship stuff you did. You want to see him or her as a person, complete with his or her strengths and flaws, then evaluate if you want to let him or her in your life again.

Being friends with your ex after breaking up differs from the other types of excuses because it has a negative aspect that is different from wanting to get back with your ex. According to Dr. Elliot, people push to remain friends with their ex because they want to keep the companionship the other person provided without having to deal with the negatives of the relationship, such as the responsibility or commitment.

If you insist that your ex should remain in touch with you to preserve the friendship, you need to examine your motivations. Do you think you can stand seeing your ex as a friend, even when he or she starts dating someone else? Are you trying to avoid the negative feelings that inevitably accompany a breakup? Even though you wanted to end the relationship, do you still want to keep ties to him or her? Are you trying to get all the positives of the relationship without any of the negatives?

On the other side, if your ex asks you to be a friend, consider whether this will be beneficial for you. Do you think your ex will value you as a friend the same way your other friends do? What do you get out of your friendships, and will your ex provide it? Do you think you can stand to see your ex date someone else and then brag to you, as his or her friend, about how well his or her date went?

If your ex wants you to be his or her friend, you have the right to say no. Your ex might in response tell you that you need to grow up, that you are being vindictive, that you are being petty, or that you are not being fair. If he or she says any of these things to you, feel free to ignore him or her. Being friends with someone should not rely on one person pressuring another into friendship. To use legal terminology, being friends needs to be a bilateral decision, with both sides agreeing to be friends. One person deciding for him or her is not a friendship.

Just in case they want to get back together

Other times, people want to keep in contact with their ex to be "available for reconciliation." The line of thinking is that if you cut off all forms of communication with your ex, you run the risk of not being available if he or she decides he or she made a mistake. How bad would you feel if he or she calls you, gets your voicemail, and decides that because you did not answer the call, you do not want to get back together?

This excuse is working in tandem with several others. You might want to be friends because you need to show him or her who you are, which will make him or her want to reconcile with you, and you need to be available for that. Or you might need to say one last thing that will completely change his or her mind about you, and when that does happen, you will need to be available when he or she decides to reconcile.

The nice thing about this excuse is how quickly it evaporates if you think about it. If your ex contacts you once or twice and decides not to reconcile with you, then he or she must not have been that serious about it. Think about what you would do if you wanted to reconcile with your ex: Do you think you would give up after a call or an e-mail went unanswered? If your ex wants to reconcile with you, he or she will get the message to you somehow.

In addition, the fact that you will not be able to move on if you keep talking to your ex needs to be repeated. If there is going to be any hope of reconciliation, it will not be during the 56th time you have contacted him or her to see if he or she is ready to reconcile with you.

I still need to have sex

Romantic relationships involve having sex. In a survey conducted from 1999 to 2002, the Centers for Disease Control discovered that 96 percent of people in America had sex by the age of 20. This has led to the phenomenon known as **breakup sex**, where couples that have broken up still remain in contact to satisfy their sexual needs. In some ways, it is understandable. After a relationship ends, people feel lonely. Their emotions are also extremely strong. Combine that with the fact that one can miss not having sex, and suddenly indulging in some breakup sex does not seem like that bad an idea, especially when you see him or her and the good parts of your relationship flash through your mind. Breakup sex has the added benefits of being safer than a one-night stand with a random stranger, and your partner has experience in satisfying you.

The problem with breakup sex is that it is a poor excuse to see your ex and exposes you to needless risks. Even if you ignore the slight possibility that you might become parents (even if you have sex with a correctly used condom, there is still a 2 percent chance you or your partner can become pregnant), or that your partner is no longer obligated to tell you if he or she is having sex with other people — meaning that your risk of getting a sexually transmitted disease has increased exponentially — you still need to face the fact that you are strengthening your connection with your ex, preventing you from moving on.

Some couples who have breakup sex claim they are simply enjoying a physical relationship free of any of the responsibilities that being boyfriend and girlfriend entail. Someone consenting to have sex with you is a benefit to knowing them, and if you only take advantage of that benefit without accepting any of the responsibilities the benefit entails, then you and your ex are just using each other to feel less empty. Eventually, it is not going to work anymore.

If you are asking yourself what you will do when you want sex then — to be blunt — you need to grow up. You are not a slave to your body's desires. You can put off eating when you feel hungry, and you can push yourself in the gym when you feel tired. You can even force yourself to go without television or the Internet when you are working to finish up a big project that is due the next day. Similarly, going through a time without sex is not going to kill you. People do it every day, and they still manage to live fulfilling lives.

We cannot avoid seeing each other

The final reason couples have for seeing each other outside the breakup is that they have to see each other. Perhaps you work together. Perhaps you have the same hobbies and the same circle of friends, or you had children in your relationship. Either way, for some reason, you cannot cut off all contact with him or her.

You win this one. You cannot realistically cut off all contact with your ex in this situation. However, you can still seek to minimize contact with your ex. If you know you are going to be seeing him or her ahead of time, then set up some ground rules. Make some guidelines about what will and will not be discussed. For instance, if you are at the same company, agree that you will only talk about business matters with him or her. If your ex refuses to discuss this with you, then you have to set up the guidelines yourself. You will not be able to control what your ex wants to say, but you can limit yourself. If your ex brings up a topic that you would rather not discuss, let him or her know. Be polite about it, but do not back down.

The same rules apply if you have the same hobbies. Do not actively avoid your ex, though. If your ex greets you, greet him or her back. If your ex asks how you are, you can tell him or her you are doing well. After that, you can politely excuse yourself. *Chapter 4 covers this topic in more detail.*

 TIME TO LEAVE

In certain situations, staying in your social circle might not be the best option. Perhaps your ex has gotten over you before you have done the same. Maybe you feel your ex is trying to lure you into fighting him or her. Maybe your ex arrives with a new boyfriend or girlfriend, or constantly brings in new boyfriends or girlfriends. In these situations, you might want to consider taking some time off from your group. If you are thinking to yourself that having to leave your social circle is not fair, you are correct. It is not fair, and it is not right. However, if your options are between leaving your social circle or being tortured on a regular basis, taking some time off from your circle of friends might be your best choice.

Before you leave, plan what you are going to do. Ask your friends if there are any groups in the area with similar interests to yours. Talk with any friends you have in other social circles and deepen your connections with them.

Make some plans so you do not spend your weekends trapped in your condominium trying to finish a marathon of television shows. Also important is figuring out when you should come back. Give yourself a month to start with. Take another month off if you still do not feel ready to return, but then return. You are retreating for your own good. You are not running away.

When you say that you are leaving, do not make a big deal about it. If someone asks, say that you wanted to try something different or that you needed a break. If you trust the person, you can admit to him or her that you need some time away from your ex, but ask him or her not to repeat that information. If he or she is your friend, he or she will not.

Chapter 4

The Ex Games

Up until now, we have talked about making a clean break from your ex. However, unless something drastic happens, like one of you leaves for a different city, the odds are good that you will see your ex again. At best, you will know ahead of time that your ex will show up, and the event will be large enough that you do not have to worry about running into him or her. At worst, you meet your ex at your favorite coffee shop, which was up to this point your retreat from the rest of the world, while you struggle to forget him or her.

What should you do when you see your ex again? How should you behave? What if your ex is actively dating again? Oddly, relationship advice glosses over this part, perhaps thinking that you will act the usual way toward someone you do not want to see — polite but guarded. The problem is that when you see your ex again, your mind puts itself into overdrive trying to figure out what topics are safe to discuss, what you can and cannot say if you want to avoid fighting with your ex, and what your ultimate goal is. If that were not enough, there is also that nagging question of how you respond if your ex decides to start pushing your buttons.

Even though dealing with your ex can feel like walking in a minefield while barefoot, it does not have to be so difficult. There are things you can do to make interacting easier.

Set Boundaries

The first thing you can do is take time with your ex and flesh out the rules of engagement for when you see each other. Make rules about what will be discussed and what will not be shared. If you work at the same company, agree to only talk to each other about business matters. This technique will work better if your breakup was mutual or at least performed civilly. Even if you cannot talk to your ex without managing to get into a fight, though, you can still draw up boundaries for yourself.

Sample boundaries are:

- Only talk about the matter at hand with your ex.

- Do not say anything about how your ex acted when you were together.

- Try not to say anything that will upset your ex.

- Avoid talking about your current relationship, or lack thereof.

These boundaries apply, regardless of where you two meet. If you go to the same martial arts dojo, practice with people other than your ex, and talk with other people before and after lessons. Do not actively avoid your ex, though. If he or she greets you, greet him or her back. If your ex asks how you are, you can say you are doing well. After that, you can politely excuse yourself.

How to Win a Fight With Your Ex

At this point, you are conjuring up mental images of your ex going through his or her catalog of best insults and verbal jabs for your next meeting. Setting boundaries and being polite are necessary, but what happens when you are with your friends and your ex makes a quick remark that you still have no fashion sense or reveals that you went through a time when you wanted to be a goth and a cheerleader, or just brings up the times you made a fool out of yourself in public. You want to answer back, and you have choice words of your own all saved up, ones that you have practiced in the mirror 20 times, just so you could get the last word in.

Do not give in to that temptation. If you get insulted or belittled by your ex, do not take the bait. As satisfying as fighting back might initially feel, this is one situation where you can only win if you refuse to fight. Your ex might be ready to make all sorts of remarks toward you, but like bullies, if your ex sees they are not having any effect, he or she is going to get tired of trying to hurt you. If you do decide to sink down to your ex's level, you are either going to get trounced because there are things you thought were off-limits that your ex has no problem bringing up, or you will beat your ex at his or her own game and look terrible in front of any onlookers — perhaps mutual friends, who are going to think your ex was right to break up with you; or your ex's new date, who will feel that your ex was right to break up with the crazy person; or your new date, who might start to put himself or herself in the place of your ex and think that going out with you again is a bad idea.

So what do you do? Keep being civil. At least one of you has to. This does not mean you have to let every insult go unanswered, though. If your ex says you tried to poison him or her with your cooking, you can point out that several people like your food. If your ex says you have terrible fashion sense, say you are sorry he or she thinks that or that you like the way you dress. If your ex brings up an embarrassing phase in your life, you can reply that everyone has an event like that in their past. Do not harp on it, though. Saying that everyone has made mistakes and then listing your ex's mistakes while dating you is not being civil — it is fighting. Your goal is to not get involved in the conflict. If this seems like too much of a cross to bear, consider this: If your ex continues attacking you or escalates his or her attacks, he or she is only going to be hurting himself or herself in the eyes of your co-workers and your social circle.

Being civil is especially important when you are talking with your ex in front of your children. Children model their behavior after role models, especially their parents. You have a responsibility to be respectful to your ex. If you and your ex fight when you see each other, your children are going to model that behavior in their relationships. Do not think they will not pick up on any subtle verbal abuse, either. Children are remarkably observant, and even if they do not understand what you are saying now, they will eventually.

Also, be civil when talking about your ex with your friends, even if your ex is not around. If you feel you must discuss your feelings with a friend, the first step is to try to keep the people who are friends with you and your husband or wife out of the conflict. Forcing your friends to choose sides is unfair to them. Second, if all the friends in whom you can confide are also friends with your ex, then it is time to gauge how trustworthy they are. Pick a friend who you know will keep your conversations confidential, and ask if you can discuss things with him or her. Make sure that nothing you say will get back to your ex. Also, avoid asking your friend if your ex has been saying anything of which you have not been aware.

Other Unhealthy Behaviors

You know how to behave around your ex, and you know how to at least act civil. Maybe you can even be genuinely polite. However, when you have to be around your ex, you are still reopening an old emotional wound — and like any open wound, it can get infected. This does not mean talking about negative emotions that are part of the healing process, such as anger or sadness. These emotions are unhealthy feelings, to the point that even if you can still manage to be polite toward your ex when you see him or her, you will not be able to move on. These emotions can sabotage all your future relationships. In extreme cases, these emotions might prevent you from having another relationship again.

Envy

The first unhealthy feeling to overcome is envy. The best description of envy comes from the researchers W. Gerrod Parrott and Richard Smith, who write that envy is an emotion "that occurs when a person lacks another's (perceived) superior quality, achievement, or possession and desires it or wishes that the other lacked it." In relationships, it is the feeling you get when you see your ex is doing better than you.

Despite what you might believe, envy is not jealousy. Whereas envy is wanting what someone else has, jealousy is a fear that someone might take away something you have, such as a boyfriend or girlfriend.

Although wanting what someone else has is not bad, the problem with envy is that it makes you unhappy, to the point where you want to inflict that pain on other people. Envy can also result in schadenfreude, or taking pleasure in your ex's misfortune.

THE GREEN-EYED MONSTER

Why do we call jealousy and envy a "green-eyed monster?" Why does someone turn green with envy? You can thank William Shakespeare for that. The earliest time jealousy is referred to as green-eyed is in the 1596 play *Merchant of Venice*, where Portia talks about "green-eyed jealousy." In his 1603 play *Othello*, the character Iago says, "O, beware, my lord, of jealousy, it is the green-eyed monster which doth mock the meat it feeds on." Because envy is similar to jealousy, it also became associated with the color green.

Other people might have used this term before Shakespeare, but he is the one who first used it. So if you come up with a clever metaphor and a friend uses it in a play, make sure he or she gives you proper credit.

Why should envy and jealousy be green, though? This is likely because the color green is associated with sickness and rot. For instance, another old saying is that someone who is sick looks a little green around the gills. Also, moldy food looks green, too. Even back in Shakespeare's time, jealousy was considered unhealthy.

Overcoming Envy

On the surface, overcoming envy seems impossible. How do you make yourself not want something? If you convince yourself you do not want something you know you wanted, are you not deluding yourself?

The truth is that when you work to overcome envy, you are not deluding yourself or crying sour grapes. Instead, you look at the reality of the situation differently and put a more positive spin on them. One of the best ways to do this is to use your feelings of envy as a motivator to achieve your goals. For instance, if your ex has a new sports car the next time you see him or her, you can use the envy you feel to spur you to start looking for a sports car of your own. If you see your ex with a boyfriend or girlfriend who looks as though he or she is a supermodel, use those feelings to drive you to get a supermodel-looking boyfriend or girlfriend of your own.

However, before you go rushing off to get whatever your ex has, ask yourself why you feel envious. Do you want a sports car, or do you want to flaunt how well you are doing to your ex? Although having a new partner who looks like a supermodel is nice to think about, maybe you are more bothered that your ex seems to have traded you for a nicer model — no pun intended. When you know the cause of your envy, you will have a clearer idea of the goal you want to achieve. Maybe getting a new sports car is something you could do without. Maybe doing well at your job and being financially stable enough that you could get a new sports car if you wanted is a better goal. As far as the supermodel, you can shoot for the stars there. You might want to consider, though, that your real goal is to find someone who makes you happy, which is the reason you become envious when you see your ex dating a supermodel.

Another way to overcome envy is to consider the positive side to not having what your ex has. So your ex has a sports car? Just consider all the money that must be leaving his or her hands monthly due to car payments and car insurance payments — money that is staying in your pocket instead of being eaten up by a sports car. If your ex is dating a man or woman who looks like a supermodel, remember that he or she is eating up all his or her free time. You, on the other hand, have time to hit the gym or write that book, or get through *Pride and Prejudice*. In other words, you can focus on you because in relationships, private time can be scarce.

Although you are thinking of the positive side to not having what your ex has, think about the positives you have. You might be extremely intelligent, for instance. You might also have an adventurous streak people lack, or you could be a skilled carpenter. Perhaps you are extremely coordinated, you have a stable job, or you have played the stock market exceptionally well. There are aspects of you that would make other people envious, too.

The final thing to consider when overcoming envy is that everyone has their positives and their negatives. Think about this — someone might be envious of you. Perhaps someone is wishing he or she had your taste in clothes, your sense of humor, or even your hair or eyes. Are you wondering why someone would ever be envious of something you possess? Chances are the person you are envying feels the same way. He or she can see the big picture about himself or herself, positive and negative, and he or she is envious of someone who has what he or she lacks. If your ex is trying to make you feel envious, think about how insecure he or she must be that he or she has to consciously try to make people feel envious. If your ex's sense of self-worth is so wrapped up in what other people think, it does not say much about his or her self-confidence or self-esteem.

When you think about envy, you realize that everyone has something enviable about them, and that everyone can be envious about something they lack in their lives. What matters is how you feel about yourself.

Bitterness

If there is one sentiment to avoid more than envy, it is bitterness — also known as resentment. You will find different definitions of what bitterness is, but in relationships, bitterness is envy mixed with anger — despising other people for what they have that you lack. Resentment and bitterness stem from a perceived unfairness, such as feeling as though your accomplishments are not being recognized, or that others are taking advantage of you. Humiliation also sparks bitterness, especially if you are publicly humiliated or if you are forced to take the humiliation without saying anything.

Just thinking about your breakup can lead to resentment, to say nothing of what happens when you meet your ex. Although becoming resentful is easy when your ex insults you and belittles you while you are trying to be civil, you can just as easily become bitter and resentful listening to your ex tell your friends about how his or her life has been since he or she broke up with you.

One of the problems with resentment is that it is easy to do. All you have to do is dwell on the events that have left you hurt and angry, and when your heart has been broken, that is entirely what you feel like doing.

Another problem with bitterness is that it will hurt you more than anyone else. The longer you stay resentful, the more you put up an emotional barrier of hostility, cynicism, and sarcasm that stops you from forming a good relationship between you and any prospective new friends or romantic interests. What is worse, bitterness can also consume you to the point where you stop growing. It can shred your self-confidence and sabotage your attempts to trust other people, as you become reluctant to reveal information about yourself to people, and it leaves you so focused on the hurt you suffered that you become unable to enjoy the present.

Effects that are even more long-term include realizing that you are lacking a purpose in life, and that your view of the world has somehow been altered so that it conflicts with what is commonly accepted to be true. For instance, if you believe in the inherent goodness of humanity, you might be surprised to discover that you live your life expecting other people will attack you if you are so stupid as to reveal too much of yourself to them.

HOW CAN YOU TELL IF YOU ARE RESENTFUL?

How can you tell if you are feeling bitter over your breakup? After all, feeling angry and sad are natural parts of the grieving process. At what point do those feelings fester into resentment? Here is a quick guide:

- Do you have to fake being happy while you are around your ex when you would rather scream at him or her?

- Do you have to police yourself to make sure you do not insult your ex or become sarcastic?

- Do you have nightmares about your ex?

- Do you get angry, seemingly without a reason?

- Do you become edgy when you start thinking about your ex?

- Do you get upset when something reminds you of your ex, such as a song, a restaurant you went to, or a certain movie?

If you find yourself nodding in recognition, you might have a problem with bitterness.

Overcoming Bitterness

Becoming bitter is easy. Getting over bitterness is less so. The first thing you have to do is want to change. Ask yourself, if you are feeling resentful toward your ex, do you feel good about that? Is it giving you any satisfaction, or is it stripping the happiness out of your day? At this point, be aware that it is hurting you. So think back to the last time you felt happy, before you started resenting your ex. Would it not be nice to feel that good again?

Would it not be nice to get on with your life and have your ex be surprised at how well you are doing, instead of the other way around? You can get there, but you have to consciously reject being bitter or jealous.

CASE STUDY: TIPS FROM AN OPRAH EXPERT

Sharon Rivkin, M.A., M.F.T., has been featured in notable publications, such as O: The Oprah Magazine, Reader's Digest, *and Yahoo.com. She has also appeared on "Martha Stewart Whole Living Radio." Here are her tips on getting through a breakup, "whether you left or were left."*

TO GET THROUGH A BREAKUP:

1. Create a good support system that includes friends and family. Assess who will be understanding, nonjudgmental, and willingly supportive, then give them a call. If there is someone who has been through something similar, put him or her at the top of your call list.

2. Seek out professional help if you can. This is a necessity if you are extremely depressed and/or anxious or terribly guilt-ridden (if you were the one who left the relationship). The more you know about yourself and your core issues, the better you will heal, learn something from the relationship, and not make the same mistakes in the next one. This is a learning experience, not a conspiracy to make you miserable.

3. Find out your core issue, for example, your "story-below-the story" from the past by using the three-step, First Argument Technique system. It reveals critical information about yourself that will help you understand the "why," the "what," and the "how" about you and your relationships. Why do I keep choosing the wrong partner? What is my past telling me that will help me with future relationships? How can I use this information to make positive changes in myself and my relationships?

4. Absorb yourself in good self-help books, and do affirmations and be grateful about what you have, rather than just focusing on what you do not have or what you have lost.

5. Remember that you are grieving and it takes time to feel good again — even if you are the one that ended the relationship. It is hard either way.

6. Look into a spiritual practice if you do not have one. This will help you look at the bigger picture.

7. If you were left, remember all the things you were not happy with. It is not all one-sided. This will help you not to feel like a victim.

8. Take care of yourself — treat yourself to a massage or facial; exercise; do whatever makes you feel better.

Take this day-by-day. Stay in the present, and do not worry about tomorrow. Your feelings and emotions about the breakup are going to be all over the place. You need all the support, information, and tools you can get at this difficult time. But know that there is a beginning, middle, and an end to this.

DO NOT:

1. Do not try to get information about your ex. You might think you want to know his or her every move, but it will only make things worse.

2. Do not have contact with your ex — less is better in this situation. If you left, do not alleviate your guilt by "checking in," and if you have been left, time and space will help you heal and get centered in yourself again.

3. Do not spend time with people who you feel are judgmental or too opinionated. You want support and honesty with compassion at this time, not necessarily advice.

4. Do not put the relationship or your ex on a pedestal. Remember the truth about the relationship and what was not working. If you left, this will help with your guilt. If you were left, this will help you feel less like a victim.

HOW TO COPE AFTER SEEING YOUR EX:

1. Know that it will stir up your feelings — good or bad — again, and it will take time to get back to your new regime of coping and getting through the breakup.

2. Call your support system to talk.

3. Once again, remember the truth about the relationship and the reasons why you have broken up.

4. Get back into present time as soon as possible. It is hard to see your ex again, but it is over.

5. Cry, scream, whatever; express your feelings. Once you love someone, you do not automatically forget him or her or your feelings. Breaking up is hard to do, so cut yourself slack if you find yourself regressing after seeing your ex.

Forget Waiting — Forgiveness is the Hardest Part

Deciding you need to move on is one thing. Doing it is another because to do so you have to forgive your ex for all the pain he or she inflicted on you, something that ranks below sticking a hand in a shark tank.

What seems so insulting about having to forgive an ex to whom you are resentful is that you know he or she was wrong. Whether your ex did inconsiderate things, such as taking your car without asking you beforehand or betrayed you by having an affair, the fact remains — if you forgive him or her, that means he or she gets away with hurting you.

First, forgiving your ex is not about doing something nice for him or her, it is about doing something nice for you. If that seems wrong, ask yourself how your ex is suffering because you resent him or her? The answer is that unless your ex cares what you think of him or her, he or she is not suffering. This gives you three options: You can spend your time resenting your ex and hoping something bad will happen to him or her; you could take matters into your own hands and make something bad happen to your ex; or you can choose to let him or her move on. The first option guarantees that you will be thinking of your ex for a long time, and the second will haunt you for the rest of your life. The third option is the only way for you to get over him or her.

So how do you forgive? On paper, it is pretty easy. You choose to forgive your ex and move on. In practice, it is harder. Forgiving someone means when you think about your ex and feel envious or resentful, you choose to let go and concentrate on other things, such as doing something good for yourself. It is not easy, and contrary to every romance in existence, there is not one moment when you forgive someone and move on. Instead, one day you wake up and realize as a passing thought that you do not resent your ex anymore, and that thought brightens your day as you head out into the world to live your life.

THERE IS NO TIME FOR REVENGE

One of the favorite concepts in fiction is someone getting revenge for a wrong. Hamlet gets his revenge on Claudius for killing his father, for example. Arnold Schwarzenegger's villains have done something that merited revenge, and the movie *The Crow* is all about a man getting revenge on the criminals who killed his wife (and him). And several romantic comedies have a villain who gets his comeuppance at the end of the movie.

Real-life revenge, though, has to deal with aftermath that fiction ignores. While the fantasy is that things go back to normal once you have exacted your revenge, the truth is that when you get revenge on someone, you might have to do things you did not think you would do. Therapist Michael Etts notes that revenge entails acts that, at best, require you to be indifferent to human suffering. At worst, it requires cruelty and the ability to enjoy someone else's suffering. Reconciling these acts can be more traumatic than the events that drove you to seek revenge, and researcher Judith Herman's 1992 research noted that post-traumatic stress disorder (PTSD) can result from revenge. There is also the problem of your ex wanting to get revenge on you after you have gotten your revenge on him or her. If your revenge is severe enough, you might also have to explain your actions to a judge.

Perhaps one of the best examples of why you should not get revenge is the University of Virginia lacrosse player George Huguely, who in May 2010 kicked in the door to his ex-girlfriend's apartment. According to Huguely, he and his ex-girlfriend had a fight. Although the details of that fight are known only to Huguely and his ex, the odds are good it involved the fact that she had broken up with him. The fight became physical, and Huguely allegedly ended up beating his ex to death. The police arrested him and he was charged with first-degree murder.

Even though forgiveness can be difficult, there are tips that can make the decision easier, or at least less hard.

You are not condoning your ex's behavior. The important thing to remember about forgiveness is that you are not letting your ex get away with his or her behavior. When you think about forgiving your ex, make sure the term does not mean, "letting him or her get away with hurting me." Instead, make sure the term means, "not letting him or her continue to hurt me." That is your ultimate goal, and it feels better to think of forgiveness that way. Forgiving your ex is about helping you to let go and move on.

Think about the best way to achieve revenge on your ex. This might seem a little contradictory, but consider this: Is the best revenge against your ex sitting around and thinking about how much you despise his or her job, significant other, and all the things he or she has that you lack? Or would a better revenge be running into your ex years later with a boyfriend or girlfriend, a job, and tastefully showing off your acquired fame or wealth? If you need another incentive, consider the fact that only one of those choices will affect your ex.

Another good way to get revenge is by making your breakup the best thing that happened to you. If you feel that your ex was trying to hurt you or was being callous when he or she broke up with you, ask yourself what will give your ex more power. Is it the view that he or she was such an amazing boyfriend or girl-friend that him or her breaking up with you wrecked your life forever? Or is it the view that your ex did you more of a favor by leaving than he or she ever could have by staying with you? Once again, the choice is yours.

Stop dwelling on the pain. Think about the past two weeks. Have your thoughts been on your ex? Have you talked with someone about how much you dislike your ex or all the ways in which he or she hurt you? The more you come back and relive the pain you have felt, the more you will resent your ex and the harder forgiving will be. To help combat this, look at the situation from your ex's perspective. Stand in front of a mirror and start to tell the narrative as your ex might have experienced it. This is not an easy thing to do, but when you try to see things from a different point of view, you are shifting your perspective and allowing yourself to empathize, even if the subject is not someone with whom you particularly care to empathize.

Realize that your ex is a person, too. While you might despise your ex, remember he or she is more than just your former boyfriend or girlfriend. Just realizing that might soften up the image you have of him or her in your head. Though — this exercise is to be used to see your ex in a different light, not to make you miss him or her again.

Look for positive signs. The more focused you are on negativity, the harder forgiving your ex will be. To counteract this, think about the positive outcomes. Granted, this can be hard when you have been stuck in a negative mindset for so long, so start small. Come up with just one positive thing that has happened as a result of your breakup. It does not have to be something big. It might just be the fact that you got to do something you liked that your ex did not, such as singing in the shower or not washing the dishes until the next day.

If you can come up with one positive, try more. Try to list 10 positive things that have happened to you as a result of the breakup. If you are having trouble, here are examples:

- Something you bought after the breakup that you had wanted for a while

- A new hobby you began

- A goal you have achieved, such as regularly going to the gym

- How much your family and friends have stepped up to care for you

- A visit you took to your favorite restaurant with your family or friends

- A new opportunity of which you took advantage

- A new project you began

- New friends that you made

- New groups you joined

- Bad habits you quit

Wish for good things to happen to your ex. Even though this might be the last thing in the world you feel like doing, try it. When you start to think about your ex and how he or she wronged you, wish him or her well. Make a habit of doing this, and you will hope that something good happens to them without feeling as though you mean the exact opposite. This trick works in part because it forces you to look at your ex in a different light, as someone who might be deserving of well wishes and not someone to be resented.

Give yourself permission to make mistakes. You already know that forgiveness is an ongoing process. You should also be aware that, like any ongoing project, there will be times when you fail to meet your expectations. You might look at the positives and dismiss them outright. Or you might wish your ex well by hoping he or she gets hit by a car, since that will teach him or her the value of looking both ways before crossing the street. Even though these are things you would not tell anyone else, after you have thought them, you might feel discouraged. Instead, be understanding. Remember that you are not perfect, that you have been angry with your ex, and that these feelings take time to get over. If you give in to feeling resentful or envious, acknowledge that you fell off the forgiveness wagon, and then make sure you keep trying. If you beat yourself up, you will be less likely to continue trying to forgive your ex. This will keep you feeling resentful. Take it easy on yourself. Try again, and remember that the important thing is to keep trying until you succeed.

A LITTLE HELP, PLEASE?

If you are not making any headway in forgiving your ex and your friends and family are not helping, you might want to consider talking with a religious leader. Forgiveness is an essential part of religions, and religious leaders in the community — such as pastors, priests, rabbis, or imams — are used to being counselors. If you do not feel comfortable talking to a religious leader, talk your issues over with a therapist or psychologist.

Stalking

No jokes or cleverness here — stalking is bad. According to Yale University, stalking is defined as "a pattern of repeated and unwanted attention, harassment, contact, or any other course of conduct directed at a specific person that would cause a reasonable person to feel fear." It is illegal in the United States. What leads to the temptation is understandable. You want your ex to know that even if he or she broke your heart, your ex cannot just pretend that your relationship did not exist, and what better way is there to do that than by constantly reminding him or her that you exist? It is a small step from reminding him or her you exist to stalking, and if you cross that line, you need to stop. Here are steps to help you.

1. The first step is to admit you are stalking someone. While you might feel that doing something as simple as going out of your way to drive by his or her house or changing your habits to shop in the same grocery store as your ex are not big deals, the fact is that people would not do this. It is one thing to feel empty without your ex and pine over losing the relationship, but when you reach the stage that you repeatedly try to see or talk to him or her, you begin to cross the line into stalker territory.

2. Figure out what to do with the time you spent stalking your ex. Like any bad habit, once a stalker decides to stop, he or she will need to let something else occupy his or her thoughts. Doing volunteer work can help, and it is also a good way for someone who has been stalking someone else to feel as though he or she is doing something to help other people. In other words, it is a good way to start feeling redeemed.

3. See a psychologist if this behavior becomes compulsive. Stalking might be a symptom of depression or a host of personality disorders, such as avoidant personality disorder, dependency, borderline personality disorder or even antisocial personality disorder. It might also be a symptom of a substance abuse problem, or a full-blown psychotic mental illness. The bottom line is that if you cannot make yourself quit stalking, then the best thing for you to do is talk with a professional.

4. When you have managed to quit stalking your ex, you need to forgive yourself. You might look back on your period of stalking your ex and wonder just what you were thinking, but do not let what you did in the past influence who you are in the present. Besides, you managed to overcome that part of yourself. You have conquered this behavior, and that says something about you.

CASE STUDY: A DATING VETERAN SPEAKS

Helen H. (last name withheld by request) is a teacher who "falls in and out of love easily," according to her. As you might expect, this has given her experiences with breakups — as the instigator of the breakup and as the person who is being broken up with. Her experiences have given her insight into coping with breakups.

Helen has a unique way of looking at healing from a relationship. "All my breakups since my heart and pride were wounded by people as a younger woman have been quite painless. I just ran off with other people and denied anybody ownership of my heart. A devious — but successful — strategy for a healthy emotional life. Contrary to what all the guidebooks tell you to do."

However, Helen's denial of ownership has led to her causing heartbreak for others, such as when she begins dating after a breakup. "I was 'preventatively' unfaithful, as it reduced my chances of heartache," she says. "If I was dishing it out then it would not hurt, and I'd justify this to myself by the thought that I would not be hurt as I had been when I was younger and more naïve."

Helen has also had to deal with her share of problems with exes, including one who has fathered her children. "I am pretty long-suffering and do not think that children should suffer for the stupidity of their parents," she says. "But I also got annoyed when my daughter's father expected to have sex with me, even though it was enjoyable. I knew I would pay for it later. He also wanted to have my house keys all the time, but did not give me his." On the other hand, Helen is quick to point out that the father of her second child, "is still my friend, and we try not to argue in front of our daughter — mostly, we succeed."

On occasions, Helen has had to be in contact with her exes after she had broken up with them. "This did happen. But I was fine with this," she recalls. "The only time it was hard was when my stomach did a lurch because I loved the person. But since the person I loved was a wonderful person, he was kind to me and friendly at work."

Not all meetings with exes have gone so well. "An Italian ex of mind was unable to come to terms with the ending of the relationship when I threw him out — physically — for the third time. I softened and let him come to visit — a terrible mistake each time. In the end, I called the police more than twice to ensure that he stopped knocking on the windows and rattling at the doors."

When advising other people on what to do to get over their relationships, Helen is clear on one point. "They should not see a shrink or therapist. There is nothing abnormal about being upset," she says. However, that does not mean she thinks someone who has gone through a breakup should not confide in anyone. "They should not hesitate to share it with their family," she says. In addition, people who have just broken up should not hold their emotions in. "They should cry, watch sad movies, and take time to be lazy for a while, not necessarily right after the breakup but sometime soon," she says.

Helen also advises people dealing with their own heartbreak to love something else, like "art, books, writing, or their garden. Start helping other people less fortunate than yourself in ways that help rather than patronize them. Get involved in politics."

Perhaps Helen's ultimate breakup advice is found in her philosophy of dating. "Partners are not supposed to give meaning to our lives," she states, "but to be friends we sleep with and have children with."

And now, a view from the other side...

Up to now, you have been reading about how to behave around your ex and how to curb your own worst impulses. Now, however, the focus shifts to your ex. What do you do if your ex starts making threats against you? What if he or she starts stalking you? What if your ex hits you in retaliation for breaking up?

Putting a Stop to Blackmail

You might not like dealing with snide comments and insults your ex makes, but you can brush them off and show your ex you refuse to let him or her hurt you. What happens, though, if your ex decides to blackmail you or threaten you?

Being blackmailed, while uncomfortable, can be solved relatively easily. If your ex attempts to blackmail you, first let him or her know blackmail is illegal. Then let your ex know that you would rather tell people yourself about the blackmail material than have him or her show it. Relationship blackmail material will be embarrassing or explicit pictures, so tell people about the blackmail materials before your ex can show them. Unfortunately, this will be embarrassing, but by doing this you take away the power they have over you and leave your ex with nothing. Just saying you will tell people about the blackmail material will be enough to stop your ex from using it.

Threats and Abuse

When your ex decides to stop insulting you and start threatening you, bring in other people. Contact your friends, alert them to the situation, and ask them to walk with you when you do errands or go out. If you believe your ex is capable of following through on his or her threats, you might want to get the police involved. According to attorney Stacy D. Phillips, though, you need to gather evidence against your ex. Save the threatening voicemails or notes he or she sends you. However, state laws prevent you from recording conversations unless you have your ex's permission.

The police should also be involved if your ex hits you. That is not just abuse; it is assault. Go to the police and file a criminal report. At the least, get a restraining order. You have heard stories or seen movies about vengeful exes and stalkers walking through a restraining order when they find out one has been placed on them, but the reality, according to Stacy Phillips, is that once people find out the law has gotten involved, they will finally be shocked back into the real world.

GUNS, GUNS, GUNS

When talking about frightening subjects like threats and violence, the issue of carrying weapons comes up. You can legally obtain a handgun, not to mention a taser, mace, pepper spray, or even a hunting knife, but what about using them? The truth is that real-life violence with weapons is almost nothing like the way movies portray it. Real-life violence with weapons is brief, confusing, and deadly. Bullets in particular are extremely lethal, and even a flesh wound is enough to take people out of a fight. If your ex decides to attack you, your biggest challenge is going to be getting your weapon out of your pocket.

Even if you manage to incapacitate your attacker, you will have to go through the legal system. If you shoot someone, you will have to deal with criminal charges, and if you survive those, you will have to defend yourself against the civil charges that your ex's family will file against you. Stabbing your ex will produce similar results. If you must arm yourself, mace or pepper spray is your best bet. It will incapacitate your attacker without permanently damaging them, giving you enough time to escape. You might want to enroll in a self-defense class if you want to make the best use of it.

When You are Being Stalked

All the advice about what to do if your ex threatens you or hits you applies equally to an ex that begins stalking you. There are more things you can do to discourage stalking, though. First, confront the stalker when he or she shows up. Tell your ex in no uncertain terms that you want him or her to leave you alone. After that, treat your ex like any other bully trying to get under your skin and refuse to talk to him or her when he or she shows up somewhere unannounced. Stalkers take any interaction as approval for what they are doing, so do not give him or her that approval. Walk past your ex if he or she shows up in your neighborhood or in your local grocery store. Return any mail or packages your ex sends you, hang up if he or she calls, and send all his or her e-mail to your junk mail folder.

You will also want to tell everyone you know that your ex is stalking you. Stalkers work best when they think they are being secretive. Letting everyone know that your ex is stalking you will take away that advantage. Also, the fact that other people know what your ex is doing will be enough to shame him or her into quitting.

If that is not enough, you might have to acknowledge that your ex might pose a threat to you. Take extra precautions. If your ex still has the key to your apartment or house, you might need to get the locks changed. You might also need to change your phone number and your daily routines. Then start collecting information and let the police know.

THE FIVE KINDS OF STALKERS

In 1999, a team of researchers led by Paul Mullen studied the different types of stalkers. From their research, they identified five categories into which stalkers fall:

- A **predatory stalker** stalks his victim to attack (meaning "rape") them.

- An **intimacy seeker** believes that she and her victim were meant to be together. She tries to create a loving relationship between herself and her victim.

- An **incompetent suitor** is a stalker who is fixated on developing a relationship, despite the fact that their victim is dating someone else.

- A **rejected stalker** is trying to rectify or avenge a divorce, a breakup, or perhaps even being fired.

- A **resentful stalker** wants to terrify and inflict mental pain on his victim, against whom he is holding a grudge.

Later research done by the National Victim Assistance Academy has come up with a sixth kind of stalker. The **vengeance/terrorist stalker** is different than other stalkers because she is looking to force her victim to do something, whether it is get involved with an extremist political party or to punish the victim for a wrong committed on the stalker.

Seeing your ex again can feel like navigating a minefield. Unlike minefields, though, you can manage to navigate through this without getting hurt. Better yet, when you are not worried about what will happen between you and your ex the next time you see her, you are free to spend all that mental effort on something truly worthwhile — improving yourself.

Chapter 5

How to Not Let Yourself Go Mentally

One of the annoying aspects of getting your heart broken is how all-encompassing it can become. Dwelling on your breakup and mentally replaying your relationship in your head to try to sort it out is natural. So is considering the ways in which you could change to win your ex back. As long as you are focused on that, however, you are not moving on. You need to take care of yourself, mentally and physically.

Your mental state is important. A negative mental state will make getting over your heartbreak harder. A negative attitude can make it impossible. On the other hand, if you can maintain a positive state, getting over your breakup will be easier. As an added bonus, it can give you stability and psychological strength that will serve you well and make getting through future crises easier. The best part is that there are ways to keep yourself mentally fit.

Self Esteem: A Primer

First thing's first — one of the casualties during a breakup is your self-esteem. There are ways that it manifests, from taking all the blame for the breakup because "I wasn't a good boyfriend" to staring at yourself in the mirror and picking out all your physical flaws. Then, there is the self-doubt that, if your ex, who knew you as intimately as your family did, rejected you, then maybe you do not have anything to offer in a relationship. Asking yourself these questions and treating yourself like something you might find in a thrift store can create mental wounds that take a long time to heal.

This problem is not helped by the fact that low self-esteem is common in American society. It is even encouraged. Americans qualify the compliments people give them, downplay their accomplishments, and berate themselves for their mistakes more than they praise themselves for their triumphs. Fortunately, there are resources available to help you patch up your self-esteem and make you feel good about who you are. Below are effective tips, emotional bandages, to help you feel better about yourself:

1. **List your strengths.** Everyone has them, including you. If you are not sure what your strengths are, ask people who know you, such as your friends or family. Your family in particular is the best resource for discovering your strengths. Find at least four or five strengths, write them down, and put the list in a safe place where you can look

at it, such as a desk drawer or the bulletin board in your home office. You might also want to make a travel copy to keep in your purse or wallet. Remind yourself of them. For instance, if you are feeling down because you cannot play basketball well, remind yourself that you have a sense of humor. If you feel depressed because you do not think you are a good writer, remind yourself that you are good at playing the trumpet.

2. **Remember that nobody is perfect.** This can be the hardest thing to do, especially if you are comparing yourself to someone who is more popular than you. Although you might be able to see all the ways in which you fall short, remember that other person has flaws too. Maybe you have not heard him or her sing because he or she cannot carry a tune with two hands and a net. Maybe he or she is bad at math or is scared of dogs. You have your strengths and he or she has his or hers.

3. **Concentrate on improving your strengths.** Think about what you can do to improve your strengths. Maybe you could write a short story or create your own stand-up comedy routine. Find a project that corresponds with your strengths and work on it. The project does not have to be big. Getting an A on the next math test is acceptable. So is making a stir-fry for dinner or cleaning your desk.

4. **Celebrate your victories.** When you succeed at something, take a moment to congratulate yourself. People succeed at a project and refuse to let themselves feel good, even for a little while because they are afraid other people might see them as being arrogant. Forget

that attitude. When you finish a project or succeed at a task, congratulate yourself. If you get an A on that math test, take time and feel good about what you did. If you baked cookies that turned out well, celebrate your baking prowess. You deserve to feel good after succeeding.

5. **Stretch your limits and impress yourself.** Do something you did not think you could do. Take a dance class, read something at a poetry slam, or even volunteer at a homeless shelter. Nothing raises self-esteem like doing something you did not think you could do. You will impress yourself, and while you are busy being impressed, celebrate the fact that you succeeded in going beyond your limits.

6. **Stay away from negativity.** People will be more than happy to take you down if they think you are not doing a good enough job on your own. It is easy to criticize someone else, and a sad truth of society is that people will rush to put you down just to make themselves feel better. During a speech in Paris in 1910, President Teddy Roosevelt had something to say about this:

> *"It is not the critic who counts: not the man who points out how the strong man stumbles or where the doer of deeds could have done better. The credit belongs to the man who is in the arena, whose face is marred by dust and sweat and blood."*

It is easier to criticize. Do not hang around these people if you can help it. Instead, make an effort to be with people who appreciate you. Your family is the best source of positive emotions and praise.

7. **Stop thinking negative thoughts.** Once you have stopped other people from unduly criticizing you, take the next step and stop thinking negative thoughts about yourself. If you keep thinking you cannot succeed or will not be a good boyfriend or girlfriend, you will not. Your negative thoughts will lead to you failing, a phenomenon known as a self-fulfilling prophecy. When you catch yourself thinking negative thoughts, first stop yourself. Take a one-minute break and calm yourself down. You might want to breathe deeply to help calm yourself. Then acknowledge that you have limitations, but also say something positive about yourself. For instance, if you are thinking that you will be a bad boyfriend or girlfriend because you get tongue-tied, admit that you do not know the right thing to say. But then tell yourself that despite being tongue-tied, you can remember important dates, such as birthdays and anniversaries.

8. **Honestly assess your weaknesses.** When you feel you have stemmed the tide of negativity in your life, you can look at yourself and honestly assess your weaknesses. However, do not let yourself be discouraged by them. Instead, acknowledge that they exist, and if they trouble you, start brainstorming ways in which you can overcome these weaknesses. If you are bad with managing money, make a commitment to yourself that you will record all your purchases at 8 p.m. every day of the week. Above all, you are working on improving your

weaknesses because it makes you feel good, not because you are worthless until you overcome your weaknesses.

9. **Learn to appreciate yourself.** No matter who you are, you do something every day that you can be proud of. Learn to spot those things and feel good about yourself for doing them. Maybe you are well organized. Maybe you paid a bill on time. Maybe you just got ironing done. No matter what it is, take time during the day and celebrate those little accomplishments.

10. **Do not expect an overnight change.** Raising your self-esteem is a process. It will take time to establish the habits of congratulating yourself and focusing on your strengths rather than your weaknesses. Do not be discouraged, though. Instead of focusing on the big picture of your self-esteem, just concentrate on the little day-to-day goals. By the time you make those goals a habit, you will be surprised at how much better you feel about yourself, and you will feel better about walking up to people and starting conversations with them.

Take a Break

As you start to get your mental state into shape, give yourself a rest. Depending on where you are in the grieving process after the breakup, you might be feeling as though you want to crawl under the covers for the rest of the day or want to move on from this grieving process at the mental equivalent of a dead run. Avoid these extremes. After all, when you have a broken leg, you do not start running as soon as the cast comes off. Similarly, you do not want to overexert a bruised ego.

First, take a break from the grieving process. At the beginning of the breakup, give yourself the time you need to feel terrible. After one or two weeks, though, give the grieving process a rest. Do something nice for yourself instead. It does not have to be something big or expensive, either. During the weekday, you can go to a nice restaurant and eat lunch, swing by a bookstore, or just take a quick run to the ice cream store. Outside work or classes, do something more substantial, like take a quick jog, get a manicure or a massage, or just go window-shopping at the mall.

Later, when you start applying the techniques in this chapter, take time out from working to improve yourself. Do something mindless, such as watching episodes of your favorite TV series or a movie. Take time out and read that book you bought. For that matter, give yourself an hour or two to just surf the Internet.

Dear Diary...

Keeping a journal can have a positive effect on your mental health, and it can help you come to terms with your thoughts and feelings and help you understand what you are feeling in the first place. When you write down your thoughts, you are giving them order instead of having them swirling in your mind. You can write down how you are angry and why, or why you feel depressed. The best part is that once you have those thoughts down, you can look over them and start making plans on how to counter them.

Your journal can also help you keep track of how you progress through your breakup. If you find yourself writing down the same problem, you can devote more time to solving it and have an idea of what works and what does not. When you start to get over your breakup, you can then use your journal to write about your goals and give yourself a roadmap for your future.

You will need...

A pen and paper. That is it. Having the paper bound will help, so get a notebook or something similar. Because this is your journal and you want to make a habit of writing in it every day, you will want to make sure that the pen and notebook are ones that appeal to you. People like to have a three-subject notebook, while others go for a leather-bound journal. People like to carry around a fancy pen, while others get by with a standard No. 2 pencil. So go shopping at an office supply store, a supermarket, or a bookstore and see what notebooks appeal to you. Then select a pen you like, and you are ready to go.

What to write about

One of the joys of journaling is that you can write about anything. If you are having trouble getting started, you can use a technique called free writing. Creative writers use it to get themselves started, and it is a valuable tool for keeping a journal.

To free write, all you have to do is have a writing prompt, a question or thought you can write about. Because you are getting over a breakup, "How do you feel?" is a prompt. So is, "How was your day today?" These prompts can keep people journaling forever. Once you start writing, do not try to compose your thoughts into perfect sentences. Any and all grammatical mistakes are permissible. So are misspellings. Do not interrupt the flow of your words to look up a word in the dictionary. The important thing is to keep up the flow of your words until you feel you are finished. After you have become more comfortable with keeping a journal, you can take a more structured approach to your journal entries if you wish. When you feel there is nothing to talk about, you can find something to say about how you are feeling.

Affirm the Positive

According to grief counselor Susan Elliott, one of the tools for helping to restore your self-esteem is using affirmations — constant repetition of positive statements. Like techniques to keep your mental spirits up, affirmation seems simple, but it will only work if you keep doing it. Affirmations, if used correctly, can be a powerful way to restore your self-esteem and give you more self-esteem than you have ever had before.

How does it work?

Affirmations affect your subconscious, the area of your mind that develops your self-image, along with your skills, habits, and other personality quirks. These aspects of your mind have one thing in common — they are made stronger by repetition. That is because your subconscious mind is simple and habitual. It takes statements at face value and does not understand anything presented to it negatively. It also only understands simple concepts, and even then those concepts have to be presented to it one at a time.

The subconscious mind takes in and imprints things that are presented to, so repeating messages to it will cause it to embrace those messages, good or bad. For instance, if a teacher in elementary school says you are intelligent and keeps repeating it, over time, being intelligent will be a part of your self-image. The same thing goes for negative messages, such as your ex berating you for being immature. Over time, you might come to believe you are immature and struggle to be more mature. Unfortunately, erasing an imprint from your subconscious is not easy. Your subconscious retains the messages it receives and the positive aspects of your self-image. It is lousy, however, for the negative aspects. However, when you realize how your subconscious works, you can figure out how to "program" your subconscious. In doing so, you can change how you think about yourself.

RISKY BUSINESS?

One of the common fears regarding affirmations and other techniques that are supposed to alter your subconscious is the idea that if you try to alter the way you think, something will go horribly wrong and you will not be you anymore. Fortunately, this fear is groundless. Affirmations are not intensive enough to do that. A fear that something like this will happen is the result of a fear of change. If you have lived with the conception that you are not self-confident, for instance, the idea of you as a self-confident person is alien to you; you start to think of people who you know are self-confident and stereotypes of what a self-confident person acts like, and you begin to wonder if your personality can survive a transformation like this or if you even want to become this new person.

Rest assured, your personality is not going to go anywhere. If anything, altering your subconscious' image of yourself will make your personality more powerful, not less. If that does not convince you, think of a personality trait you would like to change. Perhaps you want to be more responsible, or less afraid of asking people out, or less shy in groups.

Now imagine yourself as a more responsible person. Imagine yourself confidently talking to a group and having everyone's attention. Imagine that you can go up to your dream date and strike up a conversation, mentioning that you would love to talk with him or her more over dinner. After you have finished imagining, ask yourself if you were a massively different person in the scenario you dreamed up or if you were just yourself, but a more ideal version of you.

To be fair, there are techniques you should be wary of testing on yourself. For instance, while self-hypnosis is popular, you might want to discuss using it with a psychologist or physician who is familiar with the practice. You will not accidentally erase your personality while hypnotizing yourself, but get professional advice about what you are getting into.

The real problem with talking to yourself

People talk to themselves constantly, almost from the moment they get up until the moment they go to sleep. We talk to ourselves about decisions we will make throughout the day, what things we will talk about with other people, and when we are finished, we examine how we acted and assess our performance. This self-examination and self-assessment is unfavorable, bordering on cruel. We call ourselves names when we are running late, if we say something awkward, if we make a mistake on an exam, or if a work project is not perfect. "I can't believe I was late for work today," you might say. "I am such an idiot." The problem is that telling yourself this sends your subconscious the message that you are stupid, which then becomes part of your self-image.

Talking negatively about yourself is a common habit, but it is one that needs to be stopped. After all, people make mistakes. They forget to do something or arrive late or say something they should not or promise to do something they realize they cannot do. When you make a mistake, though, you internalize it and let that mistake erode your self-image. Ultimately, that leads to you feeling worthless and settling for less than you wanted, including romantic partners who are less than ideal and jobs that are less than fulfilling.

To improve your self-esteem, you have to stop with these vicious self-assessments and the constant stream of negativity. The problem, though, is that you are still going to talk to yourself. This is where affirmations come in.

What affirmations are and how to use them

Affirmations are quick bursts of positive reinforcement, sentences you can use to overwrite the negative messages you send to yourself with positive substitutes. For instance, "I am intelligent," and "I have a strong work ethic," are examples of affirmations. These affirmations fall into three categories.

The **self-soothing affirmation** strengthens the positive aspects of your self-image. This helps you feel better about yourself by drawing away attention from the negative aspects. Examples of self-soothing affirmations are statements such as, "I have a nice smile," or "I am good with computers," or even the catchphrase of classic "Saturday Night Live" character Stuart Smalley: "I'm good enough, I'm strong enough, and doggone it, people like me."

Self-soothing affirmations are ways to quell feelings of depression, anger, or anxiety, and they can also be used to counter the effects of a bad day, or to make you feel better about the work you are doing to meet your goals. You can tell yourself, "I can make it through today," or "I am handling the difficulties of the day effectively," to make it through a bad day. Statements such as, "I am getting over this breakup," and "I am discovering new, positive things about me," are affirmations that remind you the work you are doing is paying off.

Where self-soothing affirmations reinforce good feelings about yourself, **image-improvement affirmations** are designed to focus your consciousness on changes you want to see in yourself and can be used to change part of your self-image or one specific area.

Examples of image-improvement affirmations include:

- I am assertive.

- I have clean teeth.

- I have nice hair.

- I have impeccable taste in jackets.

Finally, **action affirmations** are designed to get you into the frame of mind of doing a certain action as part of a series of steps to reach your goals. You can tell yourself, "I practice juggling for a half-hour a day," if you want to be an expert juggler, or "I put 10 percent of each paycheck into a savings account," if you are working toward the goal of saving money.

Preparation: What did you just say to me?

The first step is to take the journal you have been writing in and make a new section. Then spend one day and listen to what you say to yourself. Capture the positive self-talk and the bad. You want as clear a picture as you can possibly get about what you say to yourself. What do you say to yourself as you get in the shower to start another day? What do you say when you see yourself naked in the bathroom mirror? What are you telling yourself as you drive to work, and what do you say throughout the workday and when you get home in the evening? Try to keep monitoring your observations until you go to bed, although you do not have to. The next day, look at what you tell yourself. Then, go through each negative statement and write in a positive substitute, something that addresses the same issue as the negative statement. If one of your negative comments is "I am ugly," you will need to replace it with an affirmation that says, "I look good."

The six characteristics of highly effective affirmations

When you write up your affirmations, word them so your subconscious mind will easily accept them. Think of it as though you are telling something to a small child that you want him or her to remember. Your affirmations have to be positive, personal, brief, corrective, present, and concise.

Being is vital to your affirmation sticking. Your subconscious does not understand the concept of absence, so your affirmation has to refer to something positive. This might be the reason you did not listen when your mom would say that you were not a loser or were not ugly or whatever thing the children in high school were saying about you. Eliminate words such as "no" and "not" from your vocabulary when coming up with your affirmations. If your affirmation is something such as, "I am not fat," your subconscious will remove the word "not" and instead take the meaning, "I am fat." That is not what you want. To get around this, structure your affirmation to describe what you are. "I am thin" will work. So would, "I am a healthy person." An added advantage to this is that as your mind processes this information, your conscious mind will start to be influenced by this and make you a healthier person. This is a tactic to use on bad habits you are trying to quit, such as overeating, being late, or smoking.

Examples:

- I have a nice smile.

- I am a good listener.

- I have a sense of humor.

Your affirmations also have to be personal. That is, they should connect with your needs, desires, and goals. If you write down affirmations that you got off a website or make your affirmation common, it will evade your subconscious' notice. If you want your affirmation to stick, tie it to a goal you have. "I am a person who shows up on time for movies" is a good example. Here are more:

- I am an artist who paints four days out of every week.

- I am a cook who can prepare 10 different low-calorie dishes.

- I am a writer who submits a short story every month.

- I am a salesperson who contacts 15 new clients every two weeks.

Make sure your goal is realistic, though. If your affirmation is unrealistic, you will fail to achieve your goal and will also indulge in more negative self-talk and completely negate the affirmation.

Keep your affirmations brief. After all, your subconscious is like a child. If you try to make your affirmation too long, your subconscious will start to ignore you, or perhaps only process part of the affirmation and give it a different meaning than you intended.

Make sure your affirmations are corrective. They should be encouraging you to make a change in your life. If your affirmations are reinforcing a belief you already have of yourself, you are not improving your self-image.

Present is another attribute. In the same way your subconscious does not realize the absence of something, it also does not realize anything except for the here and now. In a way, it is kind of a zen attitude. The past is gone, and the future has not happened yet. All that is left is the now. This is why your affirmations have to be phrased as something that is happening at this moment. You are not going to be anything, and you will not do anything. Instead, say what you are. Your subconscious mind will catch on.

Examples:

- I am a responsible employee.

- I am a careful mathematician.

- I am an adventurous person.

- I am someone who loves to dance.

Final, your affirmations must be concise. Going back to the analogy of talking to a child, you need to explain things in concrete terms for the child to understand them. If you tell a child to be positive, the child will have no idea what you mean. You will need to spell it out, telling the child he or she should smile and say hi to his or her friends when the child sees them. The same principle applies when writing your affirmations. Do you want to be self-confident? Then take time and think about what you mean when you say self-confident. Maybe that encompasses asking someone out that you find attractive. Maybe it means not being embarrassed when you ask for help. Your affirmations, then, can be, "I am a person who is confident when I ask someone out on a date" and "I feel good about myself when I ask for assistance."

Here are more concise affirmations:

- I am someone who reads classic literature, such as Dickens and Tolstoy.

- I am someone who swims 20 laps five days a week.

- I am someone who completes his or her project the day before it is due.

How to use your affirmations

When you have written down your affirmations, review them and then pick out no more than 12 of them. At least make sure you have seven. If you cannot come up with seven instances in which you talk negatively to yourself, do what you can and congratulate yourself for being amazingly well adjusted.

Make sure the affirmations you select represent what you want. Save the rest, though. You can come back to them after you have imprinted the first set on your psyche. What you are going to do with these affirmations is repeat them. Start your day by reading your affirmations and make them one of the last things you read before going to bed at night. During the day, read your affirmations. Try to look at your affirmations five or six times throughout the day. You can also write them on an index card and tape it in areas where you will be looking, such as next to your computer, in your locker, as a file on your smartphone, or as a bookmark. If your computer has a microphone, you can download free recording software at http://audacity.com and make an mp3 file of you saying your software. Then put it onto your mp3 player and listen to it throughout the day.

Getting these affirmations to sink into your subconscious requires days and weeks of constant repetition. So take your core group of affirmations and keep repeating them to yourself for at least a month — and not a February-sized month, even if you start in a leap year. A full 30 days is the minimum; then revisit your main list of affirmations and see if you want to add more affirmations in, take affirmations out, or even see if the current affirmations need to be revised to be brought more in line with your goals. Then go another month. Eventually, your subconscious will make these affirmations part of your self-image. Just as important, you will join the select club of people who become their own cheerleaders instead of people who constantly tear themselves down.

IS THERE NO LIMIT TO WHAT AFFIRMATIONS CAN DO?

In addition to patching up your self-esteem and boosting it to levels previously undreamed of, there are people who claim that affirmations can help you reach your goals — any goal. As in the "get into Harvard" goal or "make $1 million a year" goal. Is this true? That is not what this book is about. We are only going to use affirmations here as a tool to get you talking positively to yourself.

On the other hand, if you need something more to occupy your time, shooting for the moon will not hurt. So here is a quick tutorial on how to use affirmations to achieve any goal. First, select your goal. Any goal is good because this technique is supposed to work on anything. Then write down your affirmation, beginning with "I, [your name], will..." like this:

- I, Robert Layton, will own one of the Gutenberg bibles.

- I, Samantha Braxton, will have a savings account with more than $200 thousand in it.

Do this 15 times a day for at least six months, and you are supposed to achieve your goal, according to proponents of these type of affirmations, including Scott Adams in his book *The Dilbert Future*. The reasons for this working range from the plausible — constant repetition of a goal focuses your mind like a laser on achieving that goal and making the probability of that goal coming true much higher — to the bizarre, such as the theory that focusing your thoughts influences reality to give you what you want.

Two bits of advice if you do conduct this experiment:

1. Do not put down, "I will get back together with my ex" as your goal. You are trying to move on.

2. If you do come into $1 million, remember who told you about this technique.

I Can See the Future

Although constant repetition is a large part of affirmations, the subconscious also responds well to a positive image. This is where the technique called **visualization** comes in. Visualization increases the rate at which your subconscious absorbs the affirmations' messages, and it works even better if you can visualize while you are relaxed. Visualization is simply envisioning yourself after you have achieved your goal. See yourself being assertive, getting your way in a discussion, and feeling good about it. See yourself balancing your checkbook on a weekly basis, confident that you are in control of your finances.

One of the best times to practice visualization is right before you go to sleep. You are already unwinding after the day's events, and you can use that time to envision what you will be doing when you achieve your goal. It is a pleasant way to fall asleep. You can also designate time each week to devote to visualization. Pick an area that makes you feel relaxed and comfortable. You might have a favorite easy chair, or you can stretch out on the sofa or lie down on your bed. Taking a long, hot bath is a good option, too. Then put on soft, relaxing music, start relaxing, and visualize yourself in the future. If you recorded your affirmations, you can also break out a speaker system and set your mp3 player to continually repeat your affirmations as you relax.

Visualization has an added bonus for people who are suffering from heartbreak. It offers a built-in retreat and gives you time to indulge yourself when you feel exhausted. Plus, you are not re-treating or taking a break from reality when you visualize — you are confronting it and making sure you get the reality you deserve.

Keep Yourself Busy

Idle hands are the devil's playground and his or her movie the-ater. Breaking up with someone creates a void in your life that your ex used to occupy. As any doctor will tell you, the more you poke at an open wound, the more you are reminded it is there. The best thing you can do is to put on a bandage and let it start to heal. In the case of a breakup, you help the wound to heal by filling it with plenty of other things to get you to take your mind off your absent ex.

One set of relationship gurus, stand-up comedian Greg Behrendt and his wife Amiira Ruotola-Behrendt, say to dive head-first into your routine. Avoid the temptation to take a week's worth of va-cation and spend it in bed or watching television. Instead, go to your job and just remember that, since you are still working, your boss considers you an asset. Rejoice in that feeling. While you might not have your ideal job, you can still feel good about the fact that you are accomplishing something, even if you feel as though you are stuck in Dilbert's world. In addition to your job, keep up your other routines. Do you get a chai latte every Wednesday or go to the gym five times a week? Keep doing them. Your routines keep you going and can also be pillars of stability you can cling to in a time of stress.

It Is All About You

Outside your routines, your main criteria for keeping busy should be that it is something you want to do. Almost everyone has something they have wanted to do. Now is the time to break those dreams and goals out of storage and finally start to achieve them. Here is a list to get you started:

Goals

- Travel across the ocean to Europe or China

- Take a week's vacation in a city you have wanted to explore, such as Los Angeles or Honolulu

- Learn to speak a different language

- Learn a martial art

- Teach yourself to play guitar

- Read a book series

- Watch movies you have not gotten around to seeing

- Take college courses

Hobbies

- Teach yourself origami

- Learn to juggle

- Become an expert on antiques

- Collect coins or stamps

- Build model vehicles

- Go ballroom dancing

- Knit

- Paint

- Write (bonus points if you write a book and submit it)

- Play video games

Other

- Clean up your desk

- Organize your files

- Clean your apartment

This is about what you want to do. Although you have the same concerns about time and money that people have, you also have money you can use for your entertainment. Time to get that money out and use it. Goals, such as world travel, might take time to achieve, but planning for a long-range goal can be as rewarding as doing it, and it keeps you as busy as a hobby would.

A good strategy for keeping yourself active is to come up with two or three big hobbies or goals. You might want to mix them up. Select one long-term goal, along with hobbies, or maybe even something from the "other" category — it is alright to admit that you might have let the housekeeping go during your breakup. Then, start to figure out how to achieve it. Get yourself a sheet of paper, or even take out your journal again. Write down your three goals or hobbies, and list the next step you can take to make them happen. If you want to travel to Oslo, you might want to see when the best time is for visiting Norway. You might also want to do a quick Internet search and see what tourist attractions are in Oslo, then buy a guidebook or a smartphone app that tells you what to do when traveling to Oslo. If you want to learn a hobby, such as origami or juggling, your first step would be going to the library and checking out an instructional book on the topic or doing research on the Internet. If you want to clean your apartment, list the room that needs cleaning and then start listing what needs to be cleaned. From this point on, when you get stuck, go to those lists, look at the last thing you entered, and see if you have done it. Then, list the next thing that needs to be done. By doing this, you will be putting your mind in problem-solving mode and make achieving these goals and hobbies much easier.

EASY OR HARD?

When you are deciding on what you want to pursue, you might wonder whether pursuing easier or harder goals is better. After all, reading a book you have wanted is easier than learning how to play the guitar like Jimi Hendrix. While the rule of doing what you want to do applies to this aspect of selecting your hobbies as much as any other aspect, here are one or two guidelines. If you have had your self-esteem hit badly by the breakup, you might want to go for an easy win. You might also want to do something easy if you feel so lethargic that getting out of bed is a challenge. On the other hand, if you have too much adrenaline coursing through your system or if you still dream of shaking your ex the next time you see him or her, you might want to get involved in something more difficult, giving you another target that will let you transfer all that energy for a sustained time.

Thank You

While you are keeping yourself busy, you can use gratitude lists as a way to keep yourself thinking positively about your life. Gratitude lists are like daily vitamins, and they have the same effect, contributing to your mental well-being instead of your physical well-being.

The concept is simple. All you have to do is regularly write down something for which you are thankful. Choose a time in the morning and in the evening. You might also want to schedule in time during lunch to bolster your spirits. As for the things for which you are grateful, that is up to you. In the beginning, you might want to start small. Try something basic such as, "I am thankful for my house," or "I am thankful I am not sick." These might seem like ordinary things to be thankful for, and that is the whole point. While you are still putting the pieces of your heart back together, you can use a reminder of the things that are going well in your life. This is not going to magically make your grieving go away, but it will balance out the negative thoughts.

One of the best parts of a gratitude list is that you can keep it anywhere. If you feel disorganized, write your list on sheets of scrap paper. You can also buy a small notebook to keep with you or a little leather-bound volume if you want to be artistic. This being the 21st century, you can also take out your smartphone and type your gratitude list out as a note or series of notes. Another option is to use the Internet. Post what you are feeling grateful for on your social media account, and you will be able to see your gratitude list grow and even get encouragement from your friends.

Keeping yourself together mentally provides benefits as you go through your breakup, and it also helps to lessen those feelings of wanting to just go home and slip under the covers that people experience when confronted with a stressful situation. That is a good thing because you are going to need that extra energy for the next chapter's topic — keeping yourself physically fit.

Chapter 6

How to Not Let Yourself Go Physically

Sitting around and doing nothing during the grieving process is not doing you any good. Neither is that comfort food you have been eating. Sure, it can feel good for a day or two, but after a week you might start to notice that your clothes are getting tighter on you. Even if you ignore the health issues associated with gaining weight, looking in the mirror and realizing you have put on pounds can kill your self-esteem.

Aside from the extra weight, letting yourself go physically can drag you down in other ways. Doing nothing all day does not feel rewarding, and at the end of the day you might even be feeling depressed from seeing nothing but your four walls. Being depressed saps your energy further and leaves you feeling less like doing anything than ever, and a vicious circle is created.

Keeping yourself physically fit is just as important as keeping yourself mentally fit. It might not be what you feel like doing initially, but the better you take care of your body, the more confident you will feel after you have gotten over your breakup. It will also give you one less thing to worry about during the grieving process, which will also make keeping yourself mentally fit easier.

Where Are You Starting?

Before reading about concepts, such as eating right and exercising, figure out where you stand as far as physical fitness. This will give you a baseline, and if you feel disappointed by the results, it will give you a goal to work toward and provide you with something else you can do to occupy your thoughts as you get through your breakup. First, determine your current level of activity. What do you do for exercise during the week? Do you go to a gym, swim at a pool, or go for an occasional run? Do you spend time during the day on your feet or walking? Or is the physical part of your day when you walk to the office copier?

Second, consider your eating habits. Do you eat out? How much space do snack foods take up in your cupboards? What do you do for dinner?

Last, record your body mass index, or BMI. This number gives you a better sense of where you stand physically than just your weight. Although you might want a calculator, the formula for calculating your BMI is easy.

First, multiply your weight in pounds by 0.45.

Second, convert your height to inches. Then multiply that number by 0.0254 and square the result.

Last, divide the first number by the second. The resulting number is your BMI.

The formula looks like this:

$$\frac{(\text{weight})\text{x}.0.45}{[(\text{height})\text{x}0.0254]^2}$$

Example: A man who weighs 195 pounds and is 5-feet-9-inches wants to know his BMI. First, he multiplies his weight by 0.45 and gets a result of 87.75. He then converts his weight into inches, getting a result of 69. He multiplies 69 by 0.0254 and gets a result of 1.75. Squaring that results in 3.07. Last, he divides 87.75 by 3.07 for a BMI of 28.58.

Then, compare your BMI number against the chart below, according to the Mayo Clinic:

If your result is 18.5 or below, you are considered underweight.

If your result is between the numbers of 18.5 and 24.9, you are at a healthy weight.

If your result is between the numbers of 25 and 29.9, you are considered overweight.

If your result is 30 or above, you are considered obese.

In the example above, the subject's BMI of 28.58 puts him in the overweight category.

If you have access to the Internet, you can locate a BMI calculator. Try the one at the website of the National Heart Lung and Blood Institute at **www.nhlbisupport.com/bmi**.

Take a deep breath

After going through that quick self-assessment, your self-esteem might be dropping like a stone in a mineshaft. Before you start to panic, take a deep breath and relax. Do not worry — whatever results you got, your secret is safe. The goal here is not to motivate you to achieve that near-unhealthy level of thin reserved for supermodels, and you will not have to feel bad about your weight or exercise level. This is designed to help you get through a breakup. If you can come out the other end more fit than you did when you started, you will be able to feel more self-confident and happier with yourself and can also turn the negative of heartbreak into a positive.

Commit to Improve Yourself

Once you know where you stand physically, make a commitment to improve. If you are already in good standing physically, you can take time to reaffirm your commitment to being physically fit.

According to the Mayo Clinic, take several steps to be healthier. The first is to become more active. You do not have to run out and join a gym or start training for a marathon, but instead just schedule a half-hour into your day where you can do a low-intensity exercise, such as walking. If your schedule is too hectic to make room for exercise every day, you can get the same benefits by scheduling a longer exercise session over less days. For instance, you can put in 45-minute exercise sessions for five days out of the week, or you can exercise only three days a week if you increase your exercise session time to one hour. Three hours in one day is not going to work.

Another step to take on the path to healthier living is to be realistic about what you want to achieve. If you weigh more than 200 pounds, you are going to be disappointed if you try to slim down to below 130 in the course of two months. Instead, accept that losing weight is more like a marathon than a sprint, and your attempts to be more physically fit will go better if you lose weight at a slow and steady pace. According to doctors, the safe rate to lose weight is one to two pounds per week.

Setting realistic goals will also help you to boost your self-confidence, which is another necessary component of living healthier. If you do not feel you are making any progress when you work out, why will you continue to go? Experiment and try new things when you are exercising, such as varying the exercises you do, changing the routes you take when you go running or walking, or seeing if you look forward to exercising more when you have a friend with whom you can work out. You can also ask veteran gym members if they have any motivational secrets that make them work out as regularly as they do.

Last, the big thing to do to live healthier is to make a permanent change to your lifestyle. Living healthier is not something that happens overnight. Instead, it is a commitment you make every day. As time goes by, you might notice that you are living healthier, and that instead of reaching for a soda when you are thirsty, you grab an iced tea instead. Living healthier is also a process, which means you will have more successes one day than another, and if you eat too much junk food, the correct response is to acknowledge your mistake and try again instead of giving up.

Take a Trip to See the Food Pyramid

The first step in being more physically fit is to eat right. Not caring about what you eat is a way of life for people, and you are used to obeying your body's orders when it comes to food. Need a pizza? Eat a pizza. Want a salad? Eat a salad. Although that theory has its own pitfalls, during a breakup your body behaves differently than normal. People feel too sick to eat anything. For others, their body tells them to keep eating to appease the bottomless feeling in their stomachs. Neither extreme produces good results. Eating right will give your body the nutrients it needs and keep you feeling full without engorging yourself on calories.

The biggest problem is determining the best guide to eating healthy. While there are guides out there, one of the best comes from the Mayo Clinic, who presents its own version of the Food and Drug Administration's Food Pyramid, which is a refined version of the four food groups:

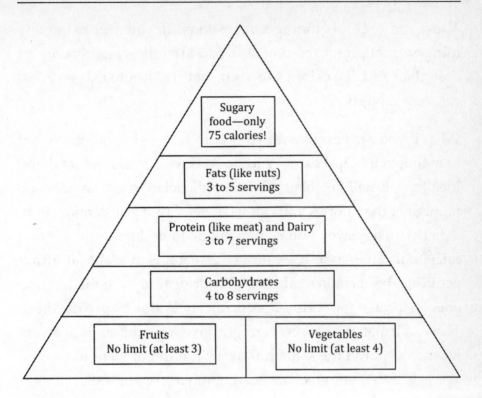

Now that you have a guide, the next question becomes, how many calories can you have? As a rule, you will need to consume 2,000 calories per day. If you want to weigh less, consume less calories. The Mayo Clinic again offers guidelines. Women who weigh more than 300 pounds should reduce their calorie intake to 1,600 per day. Women weighing under 300 pounds but more than 250 should eat 1,400 daily calories, while women who weigh under 250 pounds should eat 1,200 calories per day.

For men, if you weigh more than 300 pounds, the Mayo Clinic recommends decreasing your daily calories to 1,800 if you want to lose weight. Men weighing more than 250 pounds but less than 300 should consume 1,600 calories, and men weighing under 250 should eat 1,400 daily calories.

These are only beginning suggestions. If you feel extremely hungry throughout the day and you are following a balanced diet, then add 200 calories to your diet. Try not to exceed 2,000 calories, though.

What if you are happy with your current weight and only want to maintain it? The best way to do so is with a calorie calculator. Ideally, you will be able to talk to a dietician to get an accurate number of the calories you can have per day. If you cannot get to a dietician, however, you can go online to find a calorie per day calculator. An easy-to-use calorie calculator is available at **http://walking.about.com/cs/calories/l/blcalcalc.htm**. Another good one is located at: **http://dietforum.com/calories-per-day.htm**. These calculators, however, might give you different answers when you put in the same numbers. You might want to use the average of these numbers instead of relying on just one.

WHAT IS A CALORIE?

When talking about calories, if you eat too many, you gain weight, and if you burn more than you lose, you get thinner. But what is a calorie?

A calorie is a unit of measurement that is used to measure energy. The actual definition of a calorie is the amount of energy needed in the form of heat, to raise the temperature of a gram of water by 1 degree Celsius, or 1.8 degrees Fahrenheit. However, calories today are kilocalories, or the amount of energy needed to raise the temperature of a kilogram of water by 1 degree Celsius.

So how does this have anything to do with a person's diet? Human beings burn energy all the time. Each heartbeat burns a bit of energy, as does every other kind of muscle movement. They need a source for all this energy, and it comes in the form of food. So the number of calories a food possesses is a measure of the potential energy it will give the body.

The principle of a diet is that if you lower the amount of calories coming in, your body is not getting the necessary potential energy it needs to function. It has to siphon that energy from somewhere to survive, and it finds that energy in the stores of fat it has saved up.

One serving is how much?

To eat right, you will have to take a methodical approach to food. Break out your measuring spoons and cups, and prepare to get them dirty. As you are aware, packaged foods have nutritional information printed on the side, including the number of calories per serving. What you might not know, though, is what companies consider a serving to be. For instance, if you look at the back of a container of oatmeal, one serving consists of a half of a cup. If you have access to a measuring cup, look at how much a half-cup holds. You are going to be surprised, if only because cereal bowls can easily hold four times that amount.

Eating healthily means watching your portion sizes, and this is something that can give people trouble. Portion size is common sense. With fruits, for instance, one apple counts as one serving of fruit. So does one orange. One slice of bread counts as a serving of grains. On the other end of the spectrum, three ounces of fish or shrimp count as one serving. So do three ounces of chicken or turkey. Then there are the miniature amounts of food that qualify as a serving of fats, such as seven almonds or a teaspoon of oil.

Out of these portions, the one that gives people trouble trying to figure out how to measure three ounces of chicken, turkey, fish, or shrimp. There is a simple rule of thumb to let you know the amount of meat to get in a serving — your serving of meat should be the size of a standard deck of playing cards. So keep a deck of cards somewhere in your kitchen the next time you are preparing a meal. You might also be able to get in a quick game of solitaire while the meat cooks, if you are lucky.

Get Moving

Exercise also plays a huge role in being fit. Again, you do not need to enroll in a gym or buy a home workout station to get the advantages of exercising. Setting aside 30 minutes a day for light exercise works just as well.

When you exercise, choose something you will enjoy. If you think walking is not challenging enough, try jogging. If you want to focus more on strength training, lift weights. If you like swimming, see if there is a pool near you where you can swim laps. You might even see if there is a yoga class or a martial arts course offered nearby.

During the first times you exercise, start off slow. You do not want to discourage yourself. Then, after you have gotten into the habit of exercising, start to make the exercise more challenging. Add five more minutes to your walking time, for instance, or reduce the breaks you take while out jogging. When lifting weights, add 2 to 5 more pounds onto the amounts you started with, add another set of lifting weights, and swim more laps the next time you are in the pool. Before you know it, you will have developed a workout schedule.

A natural high

When you exercise, your body produces endorphins. The hypothalamus and pituitary gland produce these chemicals in your brain. They are the body's all-natural painkillers, and if that were not useful enough, they also act on your brain the same way opiates do. Endorphins in your mind produce a sense of well-being and a euphoric feeling that can cover up the pain your body feels. These endorphins are effective at combating negative feelings, such as sadness and anger. Endorphins are responsible for that state of being in exercise circles known as a "runner's high."

Do you have to push your body to its ultimate limits to get the effects of endorphins? No. You can get the same benefits from endorphins when you do jogging as you can when you do heavy lifting in the gym. If you push yourself to exercise too hard and for too long, you might injure yourself. Moderation when exercising is less risky, and you are more likely to stick with a moderate exercise schedule than with an intense regimen.

Can you take it?

Before you throw yourself into a workout, you might want to get a physical checkup first. While going to the doctor's office is rarely fun, it is a good way to make sure that no latent health problems will be getting in your way while you exercise. You have enough on your mind already. You do not need to deal with anything else — especially a hospital stay.

People treat a physical checkup the same way other people treat having a housekeeper clean their apartment — making sure the awful messes are hidden from sight. Avoid that urge. Ideally, bring up any health problems or concerns you might have with your doctor. Although you might feel embarrassed to bring up these concerns, you will get more benefit out of the checkup if you do.

When you get a checkup, tell the doctor why you are there, and ask his or her for any advice he or she might have about setting up an exercise schedule and any advice he or she has on easing yourself into an exercise routine. Do this and you will have one less worry on your mind as you start exercising regularly.

Date Night: Not Just for Couples

During your slow and steady path to rebuild or maintain your physical health, resolve to take one evening out of your schedule and devote it to doing whatever you want. Couples schedule regular date nights to have alone time and do something fun with someone they value. Your date nights are the same, and even better, the person you will end up appreciating more is yourself.

The first step to a successful date night is getting rid of any outside interruptions. Turn off your cellphone, for starters. Then disconnect your computer, and make sure your home phone's answering machine is primed and ready. If you have children, schedule your date night around them. When they are sleeping is a time to have your date night. If you are a night owl, have your date night after you have put your children to sleep. If you are a morning person, get up an extra hour early before your children can wake up. Whatever time you decide on, there is only one rule — make it consistent. If you stay up late on Tuesday nights, make sure you can have your date night every Tuesday. Over time, it will be a ritual you can look forward to doing, and it will give you a reason to look forward to a day in the week that is overlooked.

While you can work in the hobbies and crafts you are trying into your date night, you can also spend your time relaxing. When was the last time you had time to yourself to guarantee you could go shopping? What about the last time you could sit down and go through your book collection? What about the last time you cooked something tasty for yourself? Indulge; it does not even have to involve spending money. Perhaps you have a TV show you enjoy watching. On your date night, pop popcorn, get your drink of choice, and watch the show with no interruptions. Watching TV is something you might do every evening, but do you get to indulge in your love for a particular program?

Over time, you might want to expand on the activities you do for your date night, or you might want to develop a new routine entirely. During the spring and summer, doing an activity that takes advantage of the nice weather, such as bike riding or playing a round of Frisbee golf, is a wonderful idea. In the winter, however, you might want to find a more indoors-related activity, such as taking a class, watching movies, or working on a construction project in your workshop.

Spending time with yourself has its benefits. By indulging in something you want to do, you are giving your subconscious the message that your desires are worth listening to and acting on. Setting up a regular date night is also proof that you value yourself, and while you might have to satisfy other people's needs while you are working, there is one night a week where your needs come first.

Other Ways to Take Care of Yourself

Being healthy is not just about eating the right foods or being active. When you go through a breakup, make sure to maintain areas of your life you might not have considered before.

One of those areas is sleeping. On the average, an adult needs at least six hours of sleep per night, with the optimal amount being closer to eight hours. A study the University of Warwick did in 2010 showed that if someone does not get at least six hours of sleep per night, he or she was 12 percent more likely to suffer an early death, as opposed to people who manage to get enough sleep at night. Fortunately, the study found that sleeping more than eight hours a night did not directly affect one's chances of dying early, but it did point out that excessive sleep might be the result of a mental disorder or a serious disease. Set up a regular bedtime at night, and if you find that you cannot get to sleep, set up an appointment with your doctor.

Also, abstain from excessive drinking and recreational drug use, especially after you have broken up with someone. The main problem with using alcohol and drugs , such as marijuana, during a breakup is that being under their effects feels better than coping with your grief. Giving in to the temptation to use drugs and alcohol to avoid having to deal with your grief puts you at serious risk for becoming addicted.

Get an eye exam and a dental exam, especially if you have not had either in awhile. You are already aware that people put off getting their eyes and teeth checked for weeks if not months, but visiting your optometrist and dentist can improve your self-esteem. Aside from the obvious benefits of having up-to-date lens prescriptions and healthy teeth, knowing your teeth and your eyes are healthy will make you feel better about yourself. Plus, getting a new pair of glasses or contacts can be a good first step to reinventing your look, which is another good way to make yourself feel better physically.

People think of reinventing your look as something that only happens at a beauty salon or in an expensive department store, but that does not have to be the case. For instance, you can just get a different kind of haircut or pick up a new pair of shoes or a stylish jacket. This shows that you are not the same person you were before the breakup. Reinventing your look will also give you a needed confidence boost when you look in the mirror and see a new, confident person staring back at you.

Keeping yourself physically healthy is an ongoing process, and it is a way to keep yourself occupied as you get over your breakup. At one point, you will wake up and realize that you do not miss your ex and you look good, too.

$$\text{Chapter 7}$$

Getting Support From Others

No matter what your heartbreak is like, another person can make it easier. Having even one friend around who will listen to your complaints and help to get you interacting with the rest of the world is a valuable asset, and having a support group can ease the burden you feel.

Pride in the Name of Heartbreak

The first hurdle of getting a friend to help you is admitting you need help. This can be hard to overcome. After all, you already feel humiliated from the breakup. Admitting you cannot cope with it on your own seems like adding insult to injury. Or, you might be the kind of person who hates burdening others with your problems. These sentiments are understandable, but —

your friends are your friends because they are there for you. They are not going to feel inconvenienced because you call them to talk about missing your ex. Friends feel honored if you trust them enough to discuss your problems with them. A friend will know that you are not doing well and ask if he or she can help you. In that case, all you have to do is open up.

If you do not have a friend who preemptively asks if he or she can help and you are wondering how to select a friend to turn to, here is a helpful list of qualities to look for.

First, the friend you choose should know about your relationship and how it ended. This is not the time to reconnect with the people you knew in high school and start explaining that you feel bad you have had your heart broken. On a similar note, your friend should ideally have experienced a breakup himself or herself. If he or she has, your friend will understand what you are going through and will be more sympathetic.

Ease of communication is a big factor in determining whether you can trust someone to help you through a breakup. Make sure your friend can be easily reached, so you are not left with having to suffer through a lonely evening before your friend gets back to you the next day. You might also want to make sure your friend lives nearby, so you can hang out together when you are feeling lonely or depressed. Also, ask your friend if he or she can set aside time every day so you can talk if you need to. He or she does not have to put his or her life on hold during that time, but he or she can make sure that from 7 to 8 p.m., your friend will have his or her cellphone on or will have an instant messaging program running.

Make sure that whomever you choose to help you through a breakup is a good listener. You might be grateful for any advice you receive during this time, but unless your friend listens to what you have to say, the advice will not do you any good. Last, make sure your friend is someone who thinks you are a decent person. During a breakup you want someone who is going to listen and be supportive of you, not someone who feels the best way to support you is to help you fix all those imperfections he or she has observed.

 WHAT IF SOMEONE ASKS YOU TO HELP GET HIM OR HER THROUGH A BREAKUP?

You know how to select someone to help you get through your breakup, but what do you do when one of your friends asks you to help him or her get over a breakup? First, feel good about yourself. It says something about you as a friend and as a person that your friend trusts you to get him or her through a difficult time. Just do not let that feeling go to your head. The larger one's ego, the more difficult helping someone else becomes.

When you take on the responsibility of helping a friend get through a breakup, keep in mind simple guidelines. Your friend is not expecting you to help fix him or her. While your friend is crying into his or her pillow and asking what he or she did wrong, you might be tempted to answer. Avoid this temptation. Your friend's self-esteem is already tanking, and you do not want to add to it. Instead, just listen and be there for your friend. If he or she asks you what he or she did wrong, tell him or her that people can be wrong for each other, and the fact that your friend broke up with his or her ex does not reflect on your friend as a person.

There are exceptions to this rule. If your friend is an addict or abused his or her ex, gently suggest that he or she get professional help. Even then, do not take responsibility for fixing your friend. You are here to support.

Share your experiences with your friend. You can draw on your own breakups and tell your friend there is light at the end of the tunnel, even after that pesky freight train has finished running him or her over. Talk about what you did to get through your breakup, and make suggestions for your friend. According to relationship gurus — and husband and wife team — Greg Behrendt and Amiira Ruotola-Behrendt, just hearing that someone else went through the same situation can be a huge source of comfort.

As you are sharing your experiences, make things fun. This is going to have to be your responsibility, so when your friend needs to talk about how lonely he or she feels when he or she goes to a movie without an ex, schedule a session of Frisbee golf or a walk through the park. Doing this will help to occupy your friend's mind and show him or her that the world goes on and there is still fun to be had.

When helping a friend get through a breakup, be patient. Getting over heartbreak takes time and happens gradually, so do not expect your friend to tell you he or she is over his or her ex. This is a long-term project, but it will pay off. However, make sure you do not sacrifice your personal life to help your friend. You can set boundaries on your personal life without being a bad person. If you cannot talk to your friend while at work, let him or her know that. If you have extracurricular activities on certain days, let your friend know when they are; you can also invite him or her to join. Just make sure you set up a plan so you can be there for your friend when he or she needs to talk.

Good luck — you got through your breakup. So can your friend.

With a Little Help From Your Friends — and Family

Fortunately, you will have friends who are willing to help as you go through your breakup. You will have the support of your family, too, even if you cannot go and talk to them face to face. Having multiple friends to support you gives you more advantages, as opposed to relying on just one friend. For instance, you have more options available if you need someone to talk to. You also have a better chance of being able to hang out with someone if the first friend you call is unavailable. Last, by having a support system of friends, you have a better chance of finding someone to do an activity you want to do. If you feel that what you need to heal is to go for a run, get a friend who also likes to exercise. If your exercising friend does not like science fiction and you want to check out that new sci-fi movie, call up a friend who likes those movies. If you just want to go to the mall and shop, select a friend who is an avid shopper. Having several friends also means you can do several activities that are more fun with more people there.

Good group activities:

- Go to the beach

- Organize a local area network (LAN) party

- Play Frisbee

- Have a snowball fight

- Go clubbing

- Play a sport, such as volleyball or football

- Go to a movie

- Walk around a festival

- Go out to dinner

Family can help

Even with the support your friends give, there is nothing like being able to talk to your parents. Being able to talk to your mother or father is therapeutic, no matter how old you are. No one can love you unconditionally like your mom and your dad. Plus, who else knows you better? Brothers and sisters can be another good source of support, and close sibling relationships can be as beneficial as having a best friend around. A sibling also can support you in ways that you might be hesitant to ask of your friends, such as taking a 1 a.m. phone call to discuss what a jerk your last boyfriend or girlfriend was or letting you stay at his or her apartment for a week so you can get yourself sorted out. If you can get free time, there are worse ways to recover from a breakup than by spending time at your parents' house.

PARENT SUBSTITUTES

Not everyone has a close relationship with their parents. If you happen to fall into this category, do not worry — you likely have someone with whom you have a parent-like relationship. These can include relatives, such as an aunt, uncle, grandparent, or even an older cousin. You can also have a parent-like relationship with someone who is not related to you, such as your best friend's mother.

CASE STUDY: HOW TO LIVE THROUGH A ROUGH BREAKUP

Megan Holt is a personal trainer and grad student. Expect good things from her.

When Megan broke up with her boyfriend, she started a new job within a week and moved from Michigan to New York City. The only problem was, her ex was living in New York.

"[My ex] started talking to me again because I was close to him proximity-wise," Megan says. The fact that they had the same friends also meant that she would occasionally see her ex. "I ignored him or was reserved with him," she recalls.

Then her ex threatened her. "That's when I told him if he didn't knock it off, I'd call the cops on him," she says. "Either that, or break his arm. He left me alone for months after that."

What helped Megan get over her breakup were her friends and her family. "I got more help from them than I ever expected," she says. "They are the reason I am still here today. They were there during the late-night, tear-filled phone calls, the depression, and they have stuck by me and encouraged me as I've rebuilt my life in a better, stronger way."

Megan also changed "nearly everything" in her life. She went out with a new group of friends and began new hobbies, such as drawing, painting, and triathlons.

Still, the breakup has altered Megan's attitude toward dating. "I do not want to hurt that bad again," she states. "I have been working to overcome [that fear] by taking things slow and not letting myself get overinvested. I have yet to get into a relationship that is as serious since the breakup and, should I find myself considering it, the guy will have to stand up to multiple interrogations from family and friends." Megan has broken up with other people since her bout of heartbreak, but she says they were "far easier."

As a result of her experience, Megan has a set of standards she will not compromise on. Nothing too specific, but he has to have read more than five books in the past decade, for instance. She also has advice on how to get over heartbreak. "Don't try to stay friends — bad idea," Megan says. "It does not works. Give yourself time and distance, emotionally and physically, to heal. If, in a few years, you feel ready, then maybe give being friends a shot, but don't bank on it happening.

"Take up a healthy new hobby instead of self-medicating with drugs or alcohol — that ends poorly. Talk to your friends and family, and don't be afraid to cry on their shoulders. They'll be there for you."

Social therapy

When you are in a relationship, you talk less with your old friends as you spend more time and become more attached to your partner. This is good while the relationship is working. Unfortunately, after a breakup you might feel your selection of friends is limited, or worse, you only know your friends because your ex was friends with them first. If you find yourself in this situation, do not despair. If you used to hang out with anyone in the area, now is the time to contact them again. Tell them what is going on with minimum dramatics and ask if you can hang out with them again. The odds are good they will say yes.

However, this will not work all the time. What if you moved to a different town with your ex? What if you moved to your ex's location to be with him or her? This is where the Internet comes in. If you are like most people, you are on at least one social media website. If you have kept away from them, it might be a good time to start. Given the prevalence of social media, you have connections to your friends through the Internet. Send them a message to let them know you want to get back in touch.

If you cannot see your friends in person, you can still arrange a face-to-face webcam chat or an instant messaging chat, or just exchange e-mail.

If you like video games, you have even more options available. Current video game systems have an Internet connection with online areas where you can talk with friends if they are online. You might also find your friends online in massive multiplayer online role-playing games. People consider running around killing monsters to be a therapeutic way of dealing with bad feelings, even if the American Psychiatric Association has not formally recognized it.

Getting Professional Help

There might come a time where you realize you are not dealing well with your breakup. It might be a subtle sign, such as still missing your ex. Other times the signs might be more obvious — for instance, if you do not have the energy to get out of bed or you have no optimism anymore. If you feel you need more help than your friends and family can provide, you might want to see a psychologist.

Seeing a therapist is not a prospect that thrills people. To admit that you might need professional help in getting through your breakthrough can seem less appealing than admitting you need help from your friends, but a good therapist can help you in ways your friends might not. First, you can tell your therapist things you might be hesitant to talk about with your friends, such as the intimate details of your relationship with your ex. It can be easier to share more personal information with someone you do not know rather than your close friends, and someone on the outside can offer better advice than those who are close to the situation. A therapist can give you guidance, make suggestions as to how to heal, and work with you to help you get over your heartbreak. You will also discover that since your therapist wants you to get well, he or she will be one of your biggest supporters. There is no shame in seeking professional help.

When you decide you want to see a therapist, take time beforehand to do research. The first thing to do is see if your health insurance plan covers mental health, and if so, how much. You can get this information by calling your health care provider's service hotline. Next, do a quick search online or by using a telephone directory to locate the therapists in your area. If you live in a rural area, you might have to widen the range of your search to include the towns near you. Once you have a list of therapists, start calling them. Find out what kind of therapy they specialize in because family therapists might not be for you if you and your ex did not have children together and you are not looking for a therapist whose specialty is helping patients overcome abuse or trauma, unless your relationship was extremely bad. Other factors to take into consideration are:

- What are the therapist's hours?

- How does the therapist feel about medication?

- Is the therapist covered by your health care plan?

ASK ANGIE

One Internet resource that people have found useful is Angie's List. This website invites consumers to rate contractors, from carpenters to landscapers. Health care specialists are also covered, and you might find reviews on potential therapists by searching the website at **www.angieslist.com**.

Once you have investigated the therapists, meet them in person. Schedule an interview with each therapist and get a sense of whether you are at ease with them. If you do not understand a term they use, ask them to define it. Last, once you have decided on a therapist, schedule an appointment. On your first visit you will have to fill out forms and discuss the reason for wanting to visit a therapist, so schedule extra time for that. If you can, fill out the forms beforehand.

When you visit a therapist, think about what you want to talk about beforehand. Your therapist might instruct you to keep a journal of your thoughts for this purpose. He or she might even suggest things for you to consider between visits. While you might be hesitant to open up to a therapist at first, he or she is trying to help you. Consider the therapist as a new friend. You might not feel this way once you have to pay for your session, but it will help you talk with the therapist until then.

CASE STUDY: THE BENEFITS OF THERAPY

Dr. Talia Witkowski is a woman who knows how beneficial therapy can be for people who have had their hearts broken.

"I went through a breakup close to four years ago that almost killed me," she says. "I was in such emotional pain over the situation that I started getting back into the addictions I had sworn off in college. I spoke to everyone I could about the pain, but the more I spoke about the pain without finding any solution, the more heartache and pain I felt. I thought the only way I was going to overcome the obsession was to get the man back and propose marriage."

During this time in her life, she was introduced to Roy Nelson, a therapist. "I met him through introducing him to a patient I was treating for bulimia," she says. "The patient's mother knew of his services and asked me to make the introduction. I am so thankful that she did."

The therapy she received proved to be quite beneficial. "I spoke to him briefly about the pain of the breakup after the session with my client," Talia recalls. "When I did, the pain that I had been nursing for six months disappeared."

As time passed, Talia's relationship with Roy continued to bear fruit. "Through Roy's mentorship, I lost 60 pounds. I lost the cravings for unhealthy foods, alcohol, pot, and unhealthy sexual relationships."

One of the reasons Talia's therapist was successful was because of his ability to "crack that hard doctor shell," as she puts it. "It was a gift," she said.

Talia is doing well. She has recovered from her breakup and kicked the addictions she developed as a result. She has also lost 60 pounds, which she also attributes to the effectiveness of the therapy. "My life is completely changed on account of this special [mentor]," she says.

Types of therapy: A primer

When people think of therapists, they think of a psychiatrist's couch, talking about their dreams while the therapist sits next to them, busy taking notes. Although this type of therapy still takes place, therapists use several different types of therapy to heal their clients. Introductions to common types are provided below.

Gestalt therapy: Focuses on having the client act a certain way by engaging in role-play or acting out behaviors in front of a group. For instance, the therapist might ask the patient what he or she would say a brother if he were present or to say three positive things about himself or herself in front of a group. Or, the therapist might substitute himself or herself for someone with whom the patient is concerned and seek to provoke a conversation.

Cognitive behavioral therapy: One of the favorite methods of therapy. The National Institute for Health and Clinical Excellence in the United Kingdom favors cognitive behavioral therapy for helping to treat disorders, such as depression, bulimia, and PTSD. In this form of therapy, the therapist talks with the patient about his or her feelings, beliefs, and conclusions. The therapist then helps the patient explore the reasons behind his or her thoughts and identifies and reevaluates previous behaviors and thoughts.

Expressive therapy: Commonly uses creative hobbies to aid patients. The patient is asked to create something, whether it is a song, a drawing, or a short story, and the therapist then helps the patient investigate what thoughts and issues went into creating the piece of art.

Psychoanalysis: The grandfather of psychotherapy, which Sigmund Freud pioneered. In this type of therapy the patient's subconscious, or id, is explored. While this kind of therapy has been refined in the decades since Freud used it, the original concepts, such as the ego, id, and superego, and defense mechanisms, such as denial, are still used as models of human behavior.

Hypnotherapy: The use of hypnosis to change a person's behavior and overcome fears, stress, and anxiety.

Narrative therapy: Using this therapy, the patient talks about his or her problems and, in the process of exploring the ideas and attitudes behind them, tells the story of how those ideas developed.

Integrative therapy: A catchall category that describes using elements from different types of psychotherapy to treat a patient. While cognitive behavior therapy is the recommended type of therapy, a popular therapy is integrative because therapists tend to combine practices used in different types of therapy as they are more experienced.

Group therapy: Depends on the personal interaction found in groups to treat the patient. Interpersonal relationships are explored, and one-on-one therapies might be used. It can potentially be more effective than one-on-one therapy. Examples of group therapy are support groups and anger management or assertiveness training groups.

GROUP THERAPY? ME?

Group therapy is rarely portrayed as a positive experience, which is a shame because it offers benefits. One of the biggest is feeling a sense of belonging. If you are having trouble dealing with your heartbreak, knowing that there are other people out there who are struggling to overcome their grief can make you feel less alone. Group therapy also opens you up to people with different backgrounds than you and offers each participant different ways to look at a similar problem each member of the group has. By listening to what other people with similar problems have to say, you might discover something that will help you cope better with your issues. Group therapy allows you to try out new behaviors and experiment with new paradigms in a safe environment where people can give you feedback.

How to get the most out of therapy

No matter what type of therapy you choose, there are certain guidelines that will ensure you get the most from your treatment. If you are not motivated initially, you will be inspired to get the most from your therapy sessions once you get the bill.

When you are in therapy, one of the best things to do is be open with your therapist. Your therapy sessions are confidential and fall under the doctor-patient confidentiality privilege. You might be embarrassed at first, but this is not the time to leave anything out. The more information your therapist has to work with, the better he or she will be able to help you. If you still feel reluctant, consider this — you know you need help, and so does your therapist; otherwise, you would not be at a therapy session. This honesty includes telling your therapist about ideas you have that you feel are irrational and conflicting or about thoughts you have that disturb you, such as thoughts of suicide or violence against your ex. You might have to uncover difficult areas of your psyche to benefit from the therapy, but you might find that something you have been embarrassed about for years is not as bad as you thought it was.

During the therapy session, your therapist will offer you pieces of advice. Do not just follow his or her advice blindly. Consider it and see if it makes sense to you, and if it does not, let your therapist know. Feedback is a vital part of psychotherapy because it is the only way for your therapist to know if the treatment is having any effect. When you offer feedback, be honest, although that does not mean you have to be rude or unkind. Your therapist will take your feedback into account, although he or she might ask that you fol-

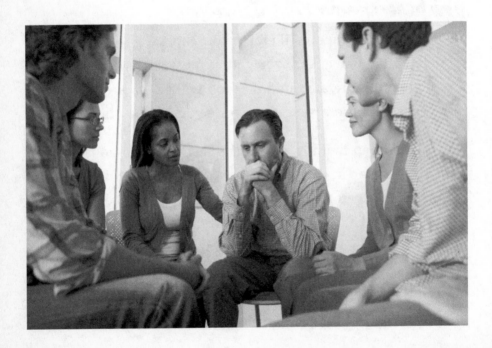

low his or her advice anyway. Therapy involves discomfort, and your therapist has a good reason for his or her suggestions.

Another important guideline is to follow the advice you get and apply it. If your therapist tells you, for instance, to keep a journal of your dreams for a week, do it. This will be applying the therapy to your regular life, which will be more effective than confining the therapy to your sessions. You will be able to discover whether the treatment is helping, and you can use the experience to give more feedback to the therapist, who can then use that information to make the therapy more effective. You are the one responsible for how well the therapy works. Your therapist will have explanations for your behavior and can offer you solutions, but unlike traditional medicine, the only person who can implement these cures is you.

When to end?

One common concern people have with starting therapy is whether they will be able to leave. After all, there is a common stereotype of people being in therapy for years, even decades. This is understandable. After all, as you talk with your therapist, you will establish emotional bonds with him or her, and people are hesitant to sever these bonds, especially with someone who has acted as a confidant for your problems. However, ending therapy is different for each person because each person comes into therapy with different problems and goals they work out individually with the psychologist. One patient might need therapy to overcome a fear of dating again because he cannot stop thinking about how hurt his last relationship left him. Another patient might need to work out the anger she feels at a partner who cheated on her. After time has passed, the therapist and patient will talk about how the patient has progressed, and if the patient and therapist agree that the patient has met his or her goals, they can choose to end the therapy sessions.

However, outside forces might end your therapy. Health care plans, for instance, limit you to a certain number of visits, or your finances might prevent you from attending regular therapy sessions. In cases like these, your therapist will determine what can be done with the amount of sessions you do have. He or she might not be able to completely heal you in that event, but he or she can at least set you on the right path.

Other types of therapy

If you cannot go to traditional therapy, you might be able to find a public support group. While support groups exist for addiction, such as Alcoholics Anonymous, support groups exist for people going through emotional difficulties, such as Codependents of Sex and Love Addicts Anonymous (COSLAA), Emotions Anonymous and Codependents Anonymous. These groups are open to new members, and you might find that they offer similar benefits to group therapy. At the least, you will be around others who know what you are going through. If you are interested in joining any of these groups, you can find them online.

COSLAA: **www.coslaa.org**

Codependents Anonymous: **www.coda.org**

Emotions Anonymous: **www.emotionsanonymous.org**

A useful group is Emotions Anonymous, which focuses on people with bad emotional problems, including people with "broken or strained relationships," according to the organization's website. Like COSLAA and Codependents Anonymous, Emotions Anonymous is a 12-step program that follows this process the American Psychological Association outlined.

- Admit that you cannot control destructive behavior or compulsion.

- Recognize that a higher power can provide you the necessary strength.

- Understand your past mistakes with the aid of an experienced member of the group, also called a sponsor.

- Make amends for the mistakes you have made to the best of your ability.

- Adopt a new code of behavior to live a new life.

- Assist those who have the same problems you have.

These are the essential goals of any 12-step program.

THE GOD PROBLEM

Although 12-step programs are popular, they have their detractors. One common criticism about groups, such as Emotions Anonymous, is that people cannot control their behaviors on their own and need the help of a higher power. While 12-step programs do not specify which higher power gives you the necessary strength, the issue remains — if you do not believe in a higher power, a 12-step program is not the choice for you. Although there are "rational" alternatives to 12-step programs that focus on overcoming alcohol and drug addiction, self-help groups for people with emotional problems are rarer. Atheists use a "natural" higher power as a substitute for deities, such as the sky or the sea, but if you have issues with believing in a higher power, your best bet might be traditional therapy.

The process

People who come to a 12-step program first have to admit they have a problem. This is from where the stereotype introduction, "Hi, my name is x and I'm an alcoholic" comes. Experienced members of the program, called sponsors, mentor new members. A sponsor is not someone who fills the role of a professional therapist, but since a sponsor has been in the same situation as the sponsee, the sponsor can help the sponsee through the 12 steps to recovery. Anyone who has made it through the 12 steps is considered to be qualified as a sponsor.

The sponsor helps the sponsee by participating in activities that are considered mentally and spiritually nourishing, such as doing artwork, reading and discussing books, or just going for a walk.

As the sponsee moves through the 12 steps, the sponsor serves as the person to whom the sponsee admits his or her shortcomings. Sponsors might also help sponsees complete the ninth step of making amends to those they have wronged. While this relationship is designed to help the sponsee, it also helps the sponsor keep himself or herself committed to the program.

Does it work?

One of the biggest questions about 12-step programs is whether they are effective at treating people. Trying to discover this is difficult due to the insistence on anonymity of 12-step programs. As a result, there are few studies performed on 12-step groups, and the number of participants is low. One of the first researchers to study Emotions Anonymous (then called Neurotics Anonymous) was Grover Boydston in 1974, whose studies have been reproduced.

Boydston's research showed that all members said they had been helped as a result of attending Neurotics Anonymous. However, being helped with a problem is different than recovering from it, and Boydston's survey of recovery results among Emotions Anonymous members seem to mirror the recovery rate of Alcoholics Anonymous members. Half of all people managed to recover, a quarter of those who joined the program recovered after stumbling and relapsing, and a quarter did not recover. Based on this study, the best advice is to try a 12-step program if you think it can work for you. If it fails, you might want to consider traditional therapy.

Chapter 8

Heartbreak and the Single Parent

If there is one thing harder than going through a breakup, it is going through a breakup when you and your ex have children. You need to cope with your own feelings and also have to counsel your children with their issues. You will also have to deal with seeing your ex on a regular basis and attempt to cooperate with him or her over issues, such as custody and child support, while trying to be a good parent to your children. If this sounds difficult, that is because it is. It does not have to be overwhelming, however. You might even emerge from the breakup a better person — and a better parent.

As a single person with children, you are not alone. Census data from 2006 revealed that 12.9 million families were single-parent families. Also according to the census, 80 percent of these families have a woman as the single parent.

A Child's Point of View

Before getting into how to cope with a breakup when you have children, first understand how children think. This requires delving briefly into the field of developmental psychology. The question, though, is which theory of developmental psychology? Is Freud's theory of development better suited to understanding the emotional stages of child development than Jung's? What about Erikson's stages of psychosocial development or Piaget's stages of cognitive development?

Here is a summary of child development, with an emphasis placed on how a breakup affects children.

From Birth to 18 months old

A child who is just born is nearly helpless. As a result, he or she quickly learns trust and dependency on his or her parents to maintain his or her well-being. Because of this dependency and trust, emotional bonds are formed that will give the child a sense of well-being and keep his or her sense of fear about the future to a minimum. Developing trust is not something that happens automatically, though. Parents must put effort into taking care of their child. Children that lack this bond of trust have problems with their emotional development later in life.

The effects of a breakup

Even infants can detect tension between their parents, but they will not be able to understand why. This tension can disrupt the bonds of trust, and as a result, the child might become edgy or nervous. They might also shy away from meeting new people as a result. To curb this effect, spend more time reassuring your child. Holding him or her is a way to lessen the tension and also spend time while you are holding your child to reassure him or her that things are alright.

From 18 Months to 3 years old

This is the stage also known as the "terrible twos," which is when children start to realize they are individuals, and they want to explore their independence. It might be exasperating for parents, but children realize they are distinct beings as opposed to their parents, and refusing to do something is part of exploring their independence. Children also learn to speak during this time. Last, they also become interested in the world around them, which leads them to taking a keen interest in exploring their surroundings.

The effects of a breakup

During this period, children might not notice tension in the household as much as infants do — they are more interested in having their immediate needs attended to. However, children have formed a solid bond with their parents by this time, and one of the parents leaving can be hard on the child. Children at this age also need to have stability and predictability in their surroundings — two things uncommon in a divorce. This is not an easy hurdle to overcome, but it can be done if parents take the time to set up routines for children at this age. Parents also need to talk about the breakup with the child and make sure he or she understands he or she is not responsible for the parents' decision to break up.

From 3 to 5 years old

At this stage, children's thought processes get more complex. They are developing a keen interest in exploring and learning about their environment and are also beginning to master language.

The effects of a breakup

Unfortunately, a parental breakup will not be any easier for children at this age. During this time, children believe they completely control their surroundings, which means they are likely to feel they are responsible in a way for their parents breaking up, and they might also react badly when they realize they cannot stop it. The best thing for parents to do is to be as open as possible with children about the breakup and model positive behavior. If children see you are adjusting to the divorce well, they will, too. Because children at that age are also becoming good speakers, talk to your child about it. Reassuring him or her that things will be alright with words and hugs is good, too.

From 6 to 11 years old

At this stage, children are introduced to peers. As a result, parents might notice that their children start to become distant from them. Because children interact with more people, they will also be exposed to viewpoints and might ask questions that are inappropriate or controversial.

The effects of a breakup

At this stage, children are aware of the effects of a breakup, but they might not understand the parents are only splitting up with each other, not the child. This can create feelings of abandonment. Children might also side with one parent over another, even when the decision to break up was mutual. During this time, parents should keep up a predictable schedule to keep the child's sense of security as intact as possible. They should also spend time discussing the situation with their child and help him or her to understand that neither parent is at fault. Again, openness is crucial.

From 11 to 18 years old

Also known as adolescence, the teenage years are where children start to become adults, focusing on establishing their own identities, stepping out of the safety nest, and shifting the focus of their lives to their friends instead of their parents. Adolescents also start to think abstractly, and they form their own opinions. This stage is not rebelling from parents but exploring and trying to find things out for themselves.

The effects of a breakup

Even though adolescents are exploring their independence and placing more emphasis on their friends, they will still be hurt when their parents break up. They might feel anger toward the situation. Their feelings might cause them to act unpredictable, from trying to rationalize blaming one parent entirely for the breakup to trying to take advantage of the guilt both parents feel over having the adolescent involved in the breakup. Adolescents will prefer to deal with these feelings on their own, but parents should be available to talk with their adolescent and provide guidance, no matter how little the adolescent might want it.

Guidelines for Breaking Up

Children need you to be open and reassuring with them when you break up with your partner. You also need to handle the duties that two people did with just one person and possibly on a reduced income. Although these obstacles can seem overwhelming, they are not impossible to overcome. The guidelines presented below will help you to get through the tougher aspects of breaking up while taking care of children.

Be open about the breakup

Repeat as often as possible. Your children will know something is going on, and by telling them instead of letting them worry and come up with their own solutions, you will help them to cope with the situation.

When you and your partner first decide to break up, talk with your children. Tell them you and your partner are breaking up (or splitting up or getting a divorce), and stress two things. First, let them know there will be changes, but no matter what happens, you and your ex still love your children and will be there for them. Stress that even if you seem distracted during the upcoming weeks and months, you are there for your children. Second, let your children know if they have any questions, you will answer them as best as you can.

Most children will need time to process the information, so be prepared to answer the questions as they come up. Because children do not follow a set timetable for when questions arise, be prepared to answer questions throughout the breakup. One common question is what went wrong. Let them know you and your partner cannot get along, even though you have tried. Do not go into specifics. Older children and adolescents might have a keener sense of what has gone wrong in your relationship, so discuss with them the value of making good choices when selecting a romantic partner.

If your children ask why you and your ex cannot work on your differences and be happy with each other, let them know that you have tried and that people cannot always get along. Again, with older children, avoid specifics, but let them know that in addition to making good choices in selecting a partner, you should also know when a situation is unhealthy and needs to change. One important thing to do while answering your children's questions is to give them hope for their future relationships.

You might want to suggest that your children visit a counselor or therapist if they seem to be taking the breakup hard. Children have bad reactions to the news that their parents are breaking up, including crying or throwing tantrums. In cases such as these, you might want the children to get the negative emotions they are feeling out of their system. If a child's reaction includes physical violence or self-harm, take him or her to see a professional therapist. However, as a parent, assess for yourself if your child's behavior is too extreme, even if it does not involve violence.

While you should be open with your children, you are not trying to get their approval for your breakup. You might feel guilty about what your children are going through as a result of the breakup, but being open with your children is not about whether you feel less guilty. It is about creating an environment where your children know it is alright to talk to you about their thoughts and feelings regarding the divorce, in addition to other things they might be experiencing, even if those emotions are negative.

A TALE OF SUCCESSFUL SINGLE PARENTING

In the early 1990s, a woman known as J.K. Rowling and her baby daughter moved to Edinburgh, Scotland, after she and her husband divorced. During her breakup, she was diagnosed with clinical depression and ended up on welfare. During this time, she worked on a novel she had begun a year or two earlier, and wrote it in a café while her daughter was asleep in a stroller beside her. After she finished the novel, she went back to school to get a postgraduate certificate of education to become a teacher. However, the book, *Harry Potter and the Philosopher's Stone*, became a huge success.

Although you will not likely become a best-selling author after breaking up, single parents can learn a lot from J.K. Rowling's example. Do not put your life on hold when you break up, continue to be a good parent to your children, and above all, do not give up. Even if you do not become a multimillionaire writer, you will still be able to take pride in yourself, and that is not something you can buy.

Do not stop being a parent

Children might act out when their parents break up. They might disrespect their parents, misbehave, or outright disobey. Parents will let their children get away with this. If you do, it could be because you have other things on your mind or that you feel guilty about what your children are going through and you feel that being lenient with your children is making it up to them somehow. Perhaps you are more lenient because you feel your ex is too strict with your children and you want to differentiate yourself or even show that you are a better parent than your ex.

Contrary to what you are feeling, be more of a parent after a breakup, and this entails being stricter. Children need predictability and stability to feel secure, and that translates into setting guidelines and limits for their behavior. When you let your children know what they can and cannot do, you are telling your children that you are in charge. This also reinforces their trust in you. If you can control you children, they will feel you can protect them from the rest of the world. On the other hand, if you let your children walk all over you, they will feel less secure and be less trusting of you to protect them.

So set limits. Make sure your children understand that you mean "no" when you say "no," and do not let them disrespect you. Make sure your children know what the limits are and that when they break the rules, there are consequences.

While you are being the lawmaker, judge, and disciplinarian, it is still alright to show your children affection. Being on your best behavior around your children is more important than ever. Children are underestimated for how much they understand, so do not say anything you do not want your children to hear if they are in the house, even if you are alone in a room. You do not know who might be within earshot. Also, avoid using euphemisms or speaking in code.

Instead, be positive and upbeat when your children are around. Children tend to imitate their parents, so this is the chance to model healthy attitudes for them. You and your children are going to be part of a new family unit, after all, so consider this an opportunity to change things in your family for the better and strengthen the family bonds.

Structure is important to a child. So is organization. To increase these aspects of children's home life, consider giving your children more responsibilities, such as doing chores. Beforehand, sit down and tell your children that everyone in the family needs to step up and help keep the house in good condition, yourself included. Go over what chores need to be done, and assign chores based on children's ages and maturity levels. You might also want to set up a chore board — a dry-erase board with magnets that show who is in charge of which chores for the week.

Responsibility does not have to mean lack of fun, though. You can also give your children responsibilities by asking for their input when creating meal plans for the week or assigning them responsibilities to help prepare for family outings. For instance, if you are going to a water park, every child might be in charge of making sure he or she has a bathing suit, towel, and footwear. One child might also be in charge of making sandwiches, while another might be in charge of getting everything in the car. You, as the parent, would be supervising and making sure everyone is doing his or her job.

RESPONSIBILITIES, CONTROL, AND LOVE

In addition to dividing up chores and having assigned responsibilities, you can make family responsibilities fun. While you can have your children suggest meals, you can also have them suggest rewards for having everyone do their chores or have them come up with vacation ideas.

Another part of being a good parent is recognizing when your child does things right. When your child does his or her chores on time, recognize and praise that, even if only through saying, "Thank you for doing your chores." Also recognize when your children do little things right, such as not slamming the door or lining up their shoes. Get into the habit of noticing when your children do things right and without help, then recognize those things and give your child genuine positive feedback. The operative word is "genuine." If your children think you are praising them to make them feel better, they will recognize it. It might also dampen their sense of accomplishment when you praise them in the future.

Last, as part of being a good parent, make sure to set aside time for your children. As you go through the breakup, you will have to deal with putting in more hours at work and dissolving your relationship with your ex, which could mean spending time with a lawyer and in a courtroom. Regardless, set aside time each week to spend with your children. Try to make family meals a regular occurrence, and on the weekends, do something fun with your children. You might all watch a movie together, go out to a restaurant, or spend time at a pool or a park. You can also use this as a reward. For instance, spend a Saturday morning raking the yard, then take Saturday afternoon off and go the beach.

In addition to making yourself available for your children all together, be sure to make time for each individual child. Talk to each of your children separately. Make sure they know you are interested. When parents break up, your children need to know that you love them and care about them more than ever, and make sure each child is receiving an equal amount of attention.

Treat your ex with respect

Perhaps the hardest part of breaking up when you have children is that you have to see your ex on a regular basis, whether you are discussing matters in an attorney's office, seeing each other in court, or just when he or she picks up the children every week. Having no contact with your ex in this case cannot be done.

Even though you have to keep seeing your ex, you can at least minimize the contact you have with him or her. This means not talking with your ex unless it is necessary. When you have to talk to your ex, you will have an easier time if you remember this simple mantra: Be professional. In other words, do your best to keep personal feelings from entering into your conversation with him or her. Treat your communication with him or her the same way you would with a business partner. This is not easy advice to follow. After all, you are still coping with the emotional fallout from the relationship, and you can come up with a few revenge scenarios or choice words you would like to impart.

Do not give in to this temptation. Even if your ex has it coming to him or her, you do not want your children to be caught in the middle. Telling your children that your ex is a terrible person will hurt them more than your ex. They love your ex, too, and this breakup does not include them. If you have to vent to someone, go to your support group and let it out. Do not be clever, either. You might think that informing your children about your ex's problems with time management or lack of a regular cleaning schedule is helping out, but your ex will disagree. It is manipulative, too.

You might have legitimate problems with your ex. This is only to be expected. When you do have disagreements, stick to certain guidelines.

Pick your battles. You and your ex will naturally disagree about certain things but refusing to give in will do more harm than good. Learn to let the little issues slide. You might think a toy is inappropriate for your child or that your ex should take your children to more than just fast-food restaurants, but you cannot control everything your ex does. If your ex tries to fight about little things, be polite but firm while refusing to engage in this behavior.

When you do have a problem, handle it with just the two of you. Do not bring your new partner into the argument, and do not let your ex bring his or her new partner in. Your children are still the responsibility of you and your ex — no one else. Talk privately, away from your children, and if you cannot find a convenient place to discuss the issue, schedule it for later. This should also give you and your ex added time to think about the issue.

If you cannot hold a civil conversation with your ex, you might need to go back to your attorney and the courts. Make this the last resort, and only for important issues, such as visitation and custody decisions and support orders.

Keep up with child support payments

If you are paying child support, you might be thinking your ex's attorney, the courts, or both, have cheated you somehow. You have not. Yes, rarely someone will end up paying more in child support than they should, but the amount you pay in child support is less than half of the expenses of raising a child. However, if you are sure your ex is somehow manipulating numbers to get you to pay more than you should, do not confront your ex on your own. Contact your attorney, go through the courts, and leave the children out of it.

If you are receiving child support, be honest about your expenses and make sure you are getting the money you are entitled to. This money is not meant for you. It is meant to raise your children. Again, if you have a problem with not receiving child support, do not confront your ex. Go through the legal system.

No matter whether you are giving or receiving child support, if you suspect that something is not right, collect evidence. Keep a record of everything, then go to an attorney or call up city hall or the local courthouse to see if your jurisdiction contains a family law facilitator. They will be happy to work with you to make sure you are being treated fairly.

Even better than going through the legal system, however, is agreeing with your ex in advance to be fair and honest about child support. By not being honest with your ex, you are creating an adversarial relationship that is going to draw in your children, and when the children get involved, no one wins.

UNMARRIED — WITH CHILDREN

Most advice given about adults with children has a bias toward the point of view that the couples are married and getting a divorce. That is not always the case, however. According to CNN, 40 percent of babies are born out of wedlock, while in 2005, the U.S. Census Bureau stated that 4.85 million couples were living together with no plans of getting married. If you are in an unmarried relationship, most of this advice applies to you the same as it does to married couples divorcing. However, be aware that establishing custody and visitation rights is harder when the couple is not married. According to the website, www.findlaw.com, although biological parents start out as full legal parents, this right can be lost. Even if you are the biological parent of a child, "exercise your parental responsibilities." This includes financially supporting the child and spending time with him or her. The court system might order you and your partner to undergo a custody evaluation, and from there, determine the extent of your visitation rights. The visitation rights are a matter of state law, rather than federal law. This part of the law is changing constantly, so if you do have to fight for visitation or custody rights, research the laws of the state you are in beforehand. Better yet, pay a visit to an attorney who does family law.

Be patient with your children when you start dating again

Although you might need time to get over the loss of your relationship with your ex, your children will also need time to get over the fact that their parents are no longer together. Your children will also need time to adjust to the fact that you might want to date again. This can be positive for you, especially if you are prone to falling into rebound relationships. Take time to get over your ex and concentrate on your family and yourself. Then, when you have moved on from your ex, get back out and start dating.

You do not have to tell your children when you start dating. It might even be a good idea if they are still dealing with their feelings of loss. You do not want to lie to them, though. Instead, say you are going out with a friend, which ideally your date should be. You will want to go slow when you do find someone you like again, though. On the average, younger children need at least a year before they will accept you bringing home a date. Older children might get through their feelings in six months, but some still require a year before they can accept you dating again. These are all averages. Find out how your children cope with the idea of you dating someone else by observing their reactions and talking to them, which you likely already do.

Waiting before you bring someone home is the best strategy for everyone, even if you are feeling impatient. If you introduce a new partner to your children too fast, they might not accept him or her and come to resent him or her for trying to be part of their lives that used to be filled by your ex. This resistance is something that might not be fully overcome. Granted, your children might not accept your new partner no matter what you do, but you can try to make the process easy for everyone by being open and honest with them.

Before introducing a date to your children, talk about the fact that you are a single parent. Stress that your children are your first priority. This might lead to a few failed dates, but it is better that your dates know now rather than later. On the other side of the equation, talk with your children and get their opinions about you dating again. Let your children know that their thoughts matter, but also keep in mind that who you date is your decision. This is a hard line to walk, and unfortunately you are on your own for this one. Keep in mind, though, that you want to make yourself and your children happy. You cannot decide to not date again because your children will be unhappy if you do. It is going to make you miserable, and you might eventually feel resentment toward your children because of it.

On a more positive note — you can also use this hurdle to show your children through your actions that someone can have a healthy, fulfilling relationship even if the previous relationship ended. Make sure your children see that your prospective partners respect them and you, and make sure you do not stand for anyone not treating you or your children well.

How to handle your ex's new partners

Your ex will want to date again, as well. In reality, your ex's partners will be your concern only at times. One of these times is before the breakup has finished. If your ex immediately starts dating and brings home new partners when he or she has your children over, feel free to mention that it might not be good for the children. Be polite and professional. If your ex refuses to let up, you might want to get a court order that says no unrelated males or females can be around the children. If you do this, do not expect your ex to thank you for your concern. Also, the order is only good until the breakup is legally finished. If you do not have a relationship that has been legally recognized, this is not an option.

When your ex starts dating again, do not let it bother you. Although seeing your ex go out with someone who is a bad parental choice can be frustrating, seeing your ex date someone can eat at your confidence, particularly if you are still trying to cope with your feelings about the breakup. At worst, you might even feel you have been replaced in the family unit.

You are still a vital part of your children's lives, though, and they need you, no matter how your ex's new partner is. Take the time you need to focus on you, and work on developing the best life you can. Make sure part of your life includes spending time with your children, and when you spend time with them, do not focus on the stuff your ex's new partner can do that you cannot. Focus on what you can do and the activities you and your children enjoy doing. If you are not good at being fashionable, focus on how good a gardener you are and develop a family garden your children. If you are not athletic, focus on playing board games with your children or go for walks.

Even if you, your ex, and your respective partners do your best to be civil, professional, and honest with one another, your children might still have problems coping with you and your ex's new partners. You can help your children get through these problems and use these problems to teach them communication skills that will minimize future conflicts.

One of the best ways to teach children how to say they have a problem is to use "I" statements, which are not as self-centered as they might sound. If your child has a problem, teach him or her to express it by saying, "I think..." or "I feel...." Then have him or her say what the problem is in the clearest way possible. For instance, your child might say, "I feel left out when you spend so much time with Larry," or, "I feel like I don't get time to see you anymore." Going back to the idea of modeling, you can use these types of statements yourself when talking to people to show your child how they work.

After you have discussed matters with your children, evaluate whether you want to bring up those problems to your ex. Arguing with your ex about his or her new partner and your children is a losing battle. Still, you might have to protect your children. Choose your battles carefully.

If the advice in this chapter has left you feeling overwhelmed, that is because being a single parent is hard. Instead of letting this drag you down, though, let it free you. Because it is hard, there is no shame in asking for help. If you can find a single parenting class, sign up for it. You can also discuss your problems with a therapist or discuss your parenting issues on the Internet. Two good places to start are **www.parenting.org** and **www.single-parentsnetwork.com**, Web communities focused on the needs of single parents. Good luck. A challenging experience does not have to break you, and will come out the other side stronger than when you began.

Chapter 9

Taking Stock of Your Life and Setting Goals

I n the middle of your breakup, as waves of anger and depression have subsided and you are left alone with your thoughts, you will ask yourself exactly what you are doing with your life. If you are like most people who have had their heart broken, the answer is,, "I have no idea." Even goal-driven, Type A people are prone to feeling a lack of direction in their lives when their relationships end. It is understandable. After all, when a relationship ends, you need time to process who you are without your ex, and people place their identity into their romantic relationships.

One is Not the Loneliest Number

When a relationship ends, one thing that haunts newly minted singles is the question of whether they will find anyone again, or whether they will live alone. If you have had these thoughts, you know what they are like — nightmares of being the fifth wheel at parties, going to movies alone, and watching as your friends pair off with other people — eventually leaving you alone, until it seems your only option is to become a recluse. Owning a house full of cats is an option.

The paradox of being mentally ready to date again is that you need to accept that being single is alright. If you feel that being alone is a curse that needs to be ended as soon as possible, you could end up falling into a trap. At worst, you might date someone who takes advantage of your desire to be with someone and uses you. You might also drive off potential dates because your desperation overshadows your good points. You might date someone who is just as desperate not to be alone, leaving the two of you in the less-than-optimal position of clinging to each other, rather than both of you evaluating the other on your merits as potential partners.

On the other hand, if you are comfortable being by yourself, you are not coming across as desperate. More important, you can evaluate people you might like to go out with on their merits, not simply being satisfied because they agreed to date you. The more content you are on your own, the better your chances at finding someone to date.

SO MUCH FOR THE HAPPY ENDING

Everyone wants a happy ending, and a common happy ending is at the end of a movie or the series finale of a TV show where the guy and the girl end up together. They do not get married all the time, but it happens enough that when the hero and heroine kiss, you feel sure that they will live happily forever after together.

The problem is that for all these TV shows and movies, the story ends when the script says it does. In the real world, the story keeps going after the cameras stop rolling. The ending is not necessarily happy. Half of all marriages end in divorce, but second marriages are more likely to fail than first marriages. Most romantic non-marriage relationships fail. This can be a demoralizing statistic to consider, but the lesson to take away from this is that love, like any worthy goal, takes work.

If you still do not accept that living alone is just as good as living with someone else, you are not alone. There are two big rebuttals people bring up when they are told they do not need a significant other in their lives. The first is that being alone is lonely. When people talk about living on their own, they talk about the silence of their homes, how boring things are without anyone else around, and the loneliness.

These problems can be solved with relative ease. First, the silence. In the 21st century, silence is more of a luxury for people than a problem. If you do not like your apartment being silent, there are options. Turning on the television is a popular fallback, or you can listen to the radio. You could also put on the headphones to your mp3 player or stream Internet radio through your computer. This can seem like a poor excuse for actual companionship, though. If you want to talk to friends, you also have several options. Use the instant messenger programs on the Internet to chat with friends, or dial up your friends and talk to them on the telephone.

Here is a list of websites and software that can help eliminate the silence and isolation.

Internet radio

- **Last.fm (www.last.fm)**: Creates a personalized radio station based on your song search.

- **Pandora (www.pandora.com)**: Creates a personalized stream for you.

- **Live 365 (www.live365.com)**: A traditional directory of Internet radio stations.

- **Shoutcast (www.shoutcast.com)**: Another directory website.

Instant messengers

- **Yahoo! Instant Messenger (http://messenger.yahoo.com)**: An instant messenger program.

- **Google Chat (www.google.com/talk)**: Another instant message program.

- **Meebo (www.meebo.com)**: Offers the ability to connect with people on multiple internet messaging programs.

- **Pidgin (www.pidgin.im)**: Allows people to connect through multiple IM platforms.

The Internet changes over time. You can also fire up your search engine of choice and search for similar websites on your own.

As far as boredom goes, it is a self-imposed condition. There are things to do on your own. Here are a few tips:

- Read

- Go for a walk or jog

- Exercise

- Swim

- Do crossword puzzles

- Browse the Internet

- Play video games

- Cook

- Watch a DVD

- Write

- Draw

- Knit

- Take a dance lesson

Come up with some more activities on your own. While you are single, this is a time for you to improve yourself or try new things. Granted, you can get a decent video game system and kill boredom with one game, which is also fun. You can also call up your friends, the ones who have patiently helped get you through your breakup, and do things with them. Organizing a movie night is a way to get people to gather at your place. So is a game night. These are also good incentives for cleaning your home, which helps to eliminate boredom with the added benefit of providing you with a feeling of productivity. You should also make it a point to get out of the house. Meet some friends for drinks, or go for a walk with them.

Be aware that living alone gives you a freedom that people in relationships do not have. Sure, you can laugh bitterly about that advantage, but consider this: When you are single, you can do almost anything you want. So eat out. Buy a movie. Plan a vacation in Europe. You do not have to wait for someone else to approve your actions, so enjoy this time and take full advantage of it. If your ex did not like mauve bed sheets, buy mauve bed sheets. If your ex hated short haircuts, get a stylish new bob and see how it looks. The only thing limiting your choices is yourself.

The second big protest is that, if you are single, you need someone to feel complete, but this is not true. You have gotten through several life experiences on your own, including passing classes, getting a drivers license, deciding on a career, and figuring out what hobbies you like. These are things you have done for yourself. So ask yourself what having someone else is going to do that you cannot do yourself.

If you agreed with the above statement, you did not mean that you literally needed someone else. You meant something more along the lines of, "I want to share my life with someone and feel loved." This takes you back to the original question: How can someone love you if you do not love yourself? At a garage sale, you get a good bargain on items the owners do not value. Love works in much the same way.

Still not convinced? Try this exercise: Take out the journal you were keeping, and write down everything you like about living on your own. Do this every day for the next week. Even if the list starts small, as the week goes by, you will be able to add more items to the list.

CASE STUDY:
DO NOT LET THE PAST
SABOTAGE THE FUTURE

Russell Friedman is Executive Director of the Grief Recovery Institute (www.grief.net) and co-author of The Grief Recovery Handbook, When Children Grieve, *and* Moving On.

We started with a rather commanding tone in the title of this essay. We said you will sabotage your future, not that you might sabotage your future, if you do not complete your romantic past.

The divorce rate that hovers around 50 percent only represents the endings of romantic relationships that marriage formalized. It does not include other romantic endings that cannot be counted. If there was an accurate account of divorces and the non-marriage break-ups, the rate would be closer to at least 60 percent.

There are two common denominators in most breakups, married or not. One is the hidden fact that either or both members of the couple were incomplete in their prior romantic relationships. That means that either or both were dragging the unfinished emotional business from the old relationships into the new one.

The second is that people bypass their intuitions and marry someone who they know is not right for them. As many as 80 percent of the people we have interacted with after their divorces tell us they knew the relationship was destined to fail, but they overrode their intuition and got married anyway.

How does this happen, given that most couples embark on their new love relationships with ardor and the best of intentions? Almost all the individuals within the new couples make a conscious decision to avoid the mistakes and pitfalls of their prior relationships.

It is wonderful to have the goal of not repeating your past, but it is another thing to accomplish that objective. Like affirmations, goals do not hold up in a crisis. You can say, "I'm magnificent and my world is filled with abundance" a million times a day, but the moment there is a crisis, you will go back to thinking you are not enough and there is no love for you, if that is your default setting.

Faced with a stimulus, which might take the form of an argument with your new mate, you will unconsciously go back to old ideas that are part of what caused your prior breakup. Your reactions will be based on obsolete thoughts and feelings about yourself that are not accurate.

Those thoughts and feelings will provoke old behaviors that did not work before and still do not work.

And many of your antiquated beliefs and behaviors relate to non-romantic relationships from earlier in life, with parents, siblings, and others. The bottom line is that many of us are dragging a boatload of emotional baggage that we define as "unresolved grief."

One of the biggest myths that affect us in our reaction to grief is that time heals all wounds. But time cannot resolve what is emotionally incomplete in your romantic past, nor can your love for someone or their love for you.

"Unresolved grief drains energy and robs choice" is a phrase that appears in our book, *Moving On — Dump Your Relationship Baggage and Make Room for the Love of Your Life.*

The truth of that quote is eminently observable in the people we have met who have been affected by a breakup and do not know how to complete what the end of the relationship has left emotionally unfinished in its wake. For many of them, it is years and even decades after a breakup and they are still devoid of energy and confused as to what to do.

"You have to let go and move on" is bad guidance. "Let go of what and move on where, and by the way, how do I do that?" Those are the questions the griever might ask that are not addressed in the poetry of "letting go."

There might be a variety of techniques that will guide you with specific actions to help you discover and complete what is unfinished for you so you can recapture your energy and restart your life. But the only method we can recommend are the ones we developed in our book, *Moving On*.

People spend decades and untold dollars in therapy and other disciplines unearthing discoveries of what they did and what they think their former mates did that destroyed their relationships.

We have met some who could [and did] write a Ph.D. treatise on their failed marriages. The problem is that discovery does not equal recovery or completion. For those analytical people, their discoveries simply add to the load they carry with them and drag into their next relationships.

Get to work immediately to discover and complete what is unfinished for you. Good, long-lasting relationships are made up of joining two whole people, not two damaged halves.

Take Stock of Your Relationship

Throughout the process of piecing your heart back together, one of your goals has been to not think of your ex and try to move on, which works about as well as when someone tells you not to think of pink elephants. After you begin to get over your relationship, though, you will want to reflect on your relationship to figure out why it did not work. Trying to figure out that answer when you have first broken up is like rubbing salt in a wound. The conclusions it leads to can also be inaccurate. You might idealize the relationship and walk away with the commitment to become exactly the kind of person your ex wanted, or you might go the opposite direction and think the big mistake you made was getting involved with your ex in the first place. Once you put emotional distance between yourself and the heartbreak, though, you can get a clearer picture of what worked in the relationship and what did not work. This is important, because you can use that information to make your next relationship better.

It might sound cheesy, but think about it — if you and your significant other got into fights because he or she always left his or her shoes out, you could assume that neatness matters to you in a relationship. If he or she got mad at you because you would leave your clothes lying around, then think about why having your shoes put away is important to you but leaving your clothes on the floor is alright. This can apply to any aspect of your relationship — did your ex like to travel while you liked to stay home? Did both of you like to go and do different things and not spend time with each other? Figuring out what went wrong helps you to figure out what kind of partner you are and what you want in a partner. You might find out along the way that you were not perfect in the relationship, either. That is alright, too. This reflection can also allow you to improve yourself as a partner.

Depending on how long you were with your ex before you broke up, you might have memories to sift through as you try to figure out where things went wrong. Granted, you might have trouble figuring this out even if your relationship only lasted months.

With that in mind, here are some questions, based on what relationship expert Susan J. Elliott formulated for you to think about as you reflect on your relationship. You do not have to answer all these questions at once. Read the questions over, think about them, and then come up with answers. Writing down the answers is not required, but it will give you time to reflect on them. Do not worry if you feel embarrassed about writing down the answers — you can always change them. Take time to answer these, but try to aim for no more than a week.

- What are six things your ex did for you during your relationship that you liked?

- What did your friends and family like about your ex? Were they the same things you liked?

- What were the positive points of the relationship?

- What were the special moments in the relationship?

- What did your family and friends not like about your ex? Did you agree with them or disagree with them? Did you make any excuses for your ex's behavior to your family?

- What were your ex's negative qualities, or qualities you wanted to change?

- What were the worst times in your relationship, not including the breakup?

- What were some of your ex's good qualities that, over time, became qualities you did not like?

- Can you think of any incidents in the relationship that should have been warning signs that you two were not getting along? If yes, what did you do about them? How did you justify staying with your ex despite these negative traits?

- Were there any problems in the relationship you can trace back to your issues?

- Is there anything in the relationship you wish you could take back?

- What do you feel your ex did wrong in this relationship?

- What do you feel you did wrong in the relationship?

- What were the times in the relationship when you or your ex hurt the other?

- If you could say anything to your ex and your ex had to listen, what would you say?

After you have had a chance to review these questions, stop. Put them away, and do not think about it. Then, go back and look at the list. Ask yourself what meant to you during this relationship and what hurt. If you come across something you no longer consider worthwhile to include, scratch it off. If something stands out to you as important, underline it, circle it or do whatever you want to make sure it stands out.

Last, try to sum up the relationship. Again, you might want to write this down to have your thoughts down. Describe what you thought about the relationship. Was it passionate or reserved? Did you like to discuss things or do more activities? Can you sum up the type of relationship you had in a word, such as sporty (playing sports or going on morning runs), academic (discussing scientific theories over coffee), physical (touching, cuddling, and sex), or geeky (going to comic book conventions together)? Then describe how you feel about your ex. Talk about his or her good and bad points. Next, write down the things in the relationship for which you were thankful, things that still make you feel mad or upset, and things you did that you think you should apologize for. Last, write down what you miss about that relationship.

Then put the paper away. Now you have a better idea of what your relationship was like and what you would like out of future relationships. This will help as you move forward into a new relationship.

CASE STUDY:
THOUGHTS FROM
A DATING COACH

As a dating coach, Loxie Gant has helped people get back up and find love again. She has written articles and has agreed to share her thoughts on getting over a breakup.

It is easy for us to pretend we are over someone, but there are unanswered questions and second guesses. Save the money you would spend on a shrink and go buy a cute new journal at your favorite bookstore. Pick up a pen before you go to bed (or whenever you are feeling sad) and write it out. The process of writing and then going back and reading it later is an amazing way to relieve that weight from your shoulders. It can even be helpful to write a faux letter to your ex that you would never give them. It helps to blow off steam and can be good for the soul.

While we are in relationships, it is easy to lose focus on the things that make us happy. Make a "Me List" of the activities, hobbies, and passions that make up who you are. Maybe even add in the things that you wish to accomplish in the near future. Write it out and then tape it on your mirror, next to your computer screen, or on the fridge. You are single, and it is time to put the focus back on you and do what you want.

Indefinite periods of time define chapters of our lives. One way to shake things up for women is to change your look or style. A simple hairstyle or hair color change might be the jumpstart you need. If you look different on the outside, you will begin to feel different on the inside. Another option is splurging on a hot new pair of stilettos to wear on your next girls' night out. This will add a spark to your strut and will guarantee a few looks at the club. In the famous words of Carrie Bradshaw, "The fact is, it's hard to walk in a single woman's shoes. That's why we need special ones now and then to make the walk a little more fun."

Setting Goals

It is good to have an idea of what you want romantically, but there is more to your life than just dating. While you are taking stock of your relationship and determining what you want in a partner, take this opportunity to look at your life and rededicate yourself to get what you want. You will want to use your journal to get the most out of this segment.

First, you need to assess where you are in life. Divide a sheet of paper into two columns, then label one side "good" and the other "bad." On the good side, write down everything you like about your life. This can include, "nice apartment," "loving parents," or "good job." Even things, such as "live within walking distance of a hair salon" or "fan of a football team," can be added. It is your list. On the bad side, list the parts of your life you do not like, such as "do not own a house," " have not traveled overseas," "am not famous," or "am not making enough money." When you are done, set the list aside and come back to it. Reevaluate your answers and make sure you have an accurate assessment of your life.

For the next step, turn to a new page in your journal. Then, over the course of the next week, list everything you would like to do in life. Do not limit yourself to only the things you think are within reach. If you want to own a mansion, write it down. If you would like to drive a Lamborghini, write it down. There are goals that do not depend on being rich and famous. You might want to be a black belt in karate, or vacation in Europe, or have a fulfilling career. Here is a sample list for you:

- Have a drawing career

- Be able to afford a sports car

- Live in Seattle, Washington

- Have a condominium with a seaside view

- Own a waterbed

- Learn to fence

- Visit Italy

- Raise two children

- Get a master's degree

Again, leave your list alone. Then go back and look at it again. Mark the items that are especially important, cross out the items that on reflection are not as important as you first thought, and if you have any new items, add them. If you are feeling organized, you might even want to arrange the goals by order of importance, creating an A-list of goals, a B-list, and a C-list. The main point once you have this list is to type it up and save it. Print out a copy and put it in your wallet. Take out the list and look at it on occasion.

Once you are finished with the list, accomplish the goals on it. This is the easiest item and the most difficult. It is easy because there are ways to achieve your goals, but it is difficult because you might be talking about achieving long-term goals, so you will have to be patient and deal with the occasional setback.

To get started on this list of life goals, select one goal. Try to make it a goal that is well defined, easy to achieve, or important to you. If you put "visit Italy" on your list, the first thing to do is gather information. How much does a trip to Italy cost? Where do you want to go in Italy? How long do you want to stay there? What will you need to have to get to Italy, other than a plane ticket? Give yourself a time limit on when you will have the information collected, then start making a plan.

One of the problems with making a plan is trying to figure out the best way to begin. Trying to figure out the best place to start can paralyze people into postponing their goals indefinitely. There is one question that can crystallize things for you. Ask yourself, "What can I do right now to get me closer to my goal?" This question automatically orients your mind to working on your goal and attacking the most immediate step. Once you have that step in mind, work on it. If you apply this to visiting Italy, you will have to do is apply for a passport, so do that. Another step is to start saving money, so put away a set amount each week. Another step is to come up with an itinerary or plan some vacation time.

Last, review your goal every day. This will keep your goal fixed in your mind and inspire you to work on it. While it might sound cheesy, one of the biggest reasons people do not achieve their goals is that they lose sight of what they want to do. Achieving a goal takes constant effort, and you will be more likely to put in that effort if you keep reminding yourself of the goal.

THE POWER OF LISTS — AND DETERMINATION

You have never heard of Zora Colakovic, which is understandable. She is not a celebrity, not a politician, and not rich. However, Zora is one of the best examples of people making a list of life's goals and sticking with it.

When Zora was a child, she wanted to be an adventurer hero. She made a list of all the skills an adventure hero would need, such as chemistry, parachuting, mountain climbing, driving evasively, archery, knife throwing, martial arts, helicopter and airplane piloting, emergency medicine, scuba diving, and demolitions.

Zora mastered the items on her list and notched incredible achievements while doing so. She applied herself in school and graduated from high school when she was 15. Three years later, she earned a Bachelor of Arts degree and completed her Ph.D. coursework when she was 21. Today, Zora is an international private investigator and bounty hunter.

She is a real-life adventure hero, like she dreamed of being when she was a child. What stands out about this story is not that Zora has racked up a list of mind-blowing achievements; rather, it is that outside this list, she is not extraordinary. Her parents were not wealthy, she does not have a Mensa-level IQ score, and she did not suffer any type of Bruce Wayne-level event in her childhood that set her on this path.

It is amazing what you can do if you want to do it.

Chapter 10

Finding and Meeting New People

You have made tremendous progress so far. Now you are starting to want to get out again and talk to people, to put yourself in a position where you can find someone else who will love you. The only question is, how do you do that?

Granted, there are people who have no problem getting out and meeting people. Even if you are a social butterfly, however, it can be hard to get back into the social scene, especially if you have spent weeks, months, or years with your ex. Now you have to walk up to people — even strangers — and try to make polite conversation with them to establish a new connection. If you are not someone who felt comfortable doing this beforehand, you might be experiencing a sinking feeling in your stomach as you realize you have to start the process over again.

Do not despair. It is not hard to get out and meet new people, and strike up a conversation. This chapter will guide you through the basics of meeting people and starting up a conversation. From there, it is up to you.

Body Language

One of the biggest barriers to conversation happens before words are exchanged. People who wonder why no one wants to talk to them have body language that inadvertently tells people to keep their distance. Although you have 10 seconds to get someone's attention when starting a conversation, you might not be aware that you only have three seconds to form a good first impression. Just by looking at your body language, another person will be able to immediately tell if you are approachable for conversation or if you would rather be left alone. Make sure you are not wearing clashing colors; body language plays a bigger role in making a first impression. According to several studies, the latest one Hickson, Stacks, and Moore performed in 2004, nonverbal communication amounts for anywhere from 63 percent to 93 percent of the information transmitted while talking.

Nonverbal communication is rule-based, and the rules vary with each culture. Americans are unlikely to grasp the subtleties of the Japanese bow, and Italians who visit the United States learn that Americans have a wider area of personal space than Italians. Even if you think that the subtleties of non-verbal communication are not worth memorizing, odds are that you shake hands with someone you meet for the first time and dress nicely for Thanksgiving dinner. When you wear a T-shirt and jeans to a rock concert, you are engaging in nonverbal communication.

Nonverbal communication is ingrained and performed unconsciously, so the good news is that you can intentionally use nonverbal communication to make yourself appear friendly, sociable, and a good listener. Just as you can select the kind of clothes that will make the best impression at an interview, you can employ body language that will make people want to come and talk to you.

Good body language is open and inviting and makes people more receptive to the idea of going up and talking to you. Despite the name, body language is not a new language to be mastered, like sign language. Everyone uses body language, whether they realize it or not. When you smile while watching television, for instance, you are communicating that you are happy about the show being broadcast. When you scowl at the cup you are holding, you are signaling that you do not like the taste of the coffee.

All you have to do to create body language that invites communication is to be aware of five or six simple techniques.

Smile to be approachable

The first technique is the easiest — smile. Smiling indicates friendliness, implies openness to meeting other people, and sends out a nonverbal invitation for other people to smile back. If that were not enough of a draw for other people, a smile is also an implied compliment. So the next time you are at a party and see someone you want to talk with, simply smile at them.

Frowning, on the other hand, is a warning message. So is looking serious or deep in thought. When you are frowning or looking deep in thought, you are giving off signals that you do not want anyone to talk to you.

How should you smile at someone? After studying smiling techniques, conversationalist Leil Lowndes came up with one method she believes trumps the rest. When you see someone, do not immediately break into a smile. Instead, stare at the person for a second. Take their measure, as your grandparents might have said. Then let a smile spread across your face. This works better than flashing a quick smile at someone because it gives the other person the impression that your smile is meant exclusively for him or her. It is a flattering assumption, and it will make him or her feel good about talking to you as long as the conversation lasts.

Keep your chin up

A corollary to smiling is to keep your chin up, which lets that smile you are wearing be broadcast to the rest of the crowd and makes you appear more confident. Here is a quick study — the next time you are at party or a business function, look at the most charismatic people in the room. You will see that their chins are up, and they are welcoming all conversation.

A good way to practice keeping your chin up is to look at the foreheads of other people in the room. The natural inclination for most people is to keep their eyes at eye level, but staring at forehead level has a difference most people cannot detect. It will keep your chin up and make your smile more inviting. As an added bonus, it will also make you appear more confident, which is attractive to people looking for someone to engage in conversation.

Welcome them with open arms

Another nonverbal signal that shows you are approachable is having your arms open. Although crossing your arms might be comfortable, it sends out a strong signal to the rest of the world that you are annoyed or angry. Drop your arms to your sides or have an excuse to keep them away from your body. You will be sending out a cannot-miss, nonverbal, welcoming gesture.

This information can seem counterintuitive. Some people try to get others to approach them by looking as though they are lost in thought or pondering the truths of the universe. This posture entails crossing one's arms or putting a hand to one's chin. The hope is that someone will approach and ask what you are think-ing about, and a deep, meaningful conversation can ensue based on the initial deep thought. This posture has the opposite effect — people will assume you are thinking about something, but they will not want to interrupt you because you are thinking.

The habit of crossing your arms can be strong. To break it, keep one hand occupied. Get a drink and carry it around, or get a small plate of hors d'oeuvres. Women have an advantage here if they have a small strapless purse, which they can use the same way as a drink to stop their arms from crossing. You might also try to prevent your arms from crossing by sticking your hands in your pants pocket, but that will trap your arms to your sides and sig-nal that you are closed off.

Other tricks for keeping your arms open include:

- Hitching your thumbs to your belt loops (popular among cowboys and in the country)

- Draping your jacket over one arm (this works best when outdoors)

- Putting a hand on your hip (this is mostly for women)

- Carrying a pen (also a conversation starter)

Carrying a drink is also beneficial because it leads into the next technique for good body language: touch. Although excessive touching is frowned on in society, also consider some initial touching polite, especially in the form of a handshake. The next time you go to talk to someone, stick out your hand and offer it for the other person to shake. They will naturally respond with their corresponding hand, and you will have made a connection.

Once you have established that you are receptive to talking with someone, focus on body language that lets people know you are interested in what they have to say. This can be accomplished by something as simple as leaning forward. When you are sitting next to another person who is talking to you, leaning forward indicates that you are interested in the other person and what he or she is saying. It encourages the other person to keep talking, secure in the knowledge that you appreciate what he or she is talking about. This can be counterintuitive for most people, who like to lean back while talking to someone else, especially during long conversations, to relax. However, this posture signals to your conversation partner that you are not interested in what he or she has to say or that you are not taking what he or she has to say seriously.

When you are leaning forward, do not lean in far. At best, it will look awkward, and at worst, you will be invading the other person's personal space. Sit or stand with your back straight, to start with. From there, lean forward. Practice this by yourself to have this posture look natural. If you are at a table with someone else, you are in luck. Instead of worrying how far too far is, lean forward and rest on your arms to signify interest.

During a conversation, also nod occasionally to show understanding and agreement. Nodding also signals approval, so the person you are talking to will feel that you approve of what he or she is saying. However, moderate your nodding. You do not want to come off looking like a Bobblehead.

THE GOOD BODY LANGUAGE GUIDE

- Smile at people.

- Keep your arms open and inviting.

- Shake hands to establish physical contact.

- Lean forward while someone is talking to show you are interested.

- Nod occasionally.

- Keep eye contact — but do not overdo it.

Ritual Questions and Conversation Starters

The easiest way to get someone's attention is through a "ritual" question, also known as an icebreaker — a tried-and-true method of getting a quick piece of information that also communicates a desire to learn more about the person to whom you are talking. There are three types of ritual questions, which can easily draw another person into a conversation.

The first type of ritual question works by noticing something the person is carrying, such as a book, pet, or sport or fashion accessory. Ask a ritual question that requires the other person to give you some information that relates to that item, such as, "Where did you get your dog?" or "Where do you play tennis?"

These questions can be applied to anything the person is carrying. Some items, such as musical instruments, are an invitation to ask the person how long they have been playing, the kind of music they like to play, and their favorite artist. Other items, such as photographs, are more subtle because they are more personal to the person. Regardless, asking a ritual question based on something someone is carrying is not meant to pry or obtain information. It is a way to show interest in the person.

A second type of ritual question depends on the situation you find yourselves in. If you are at a dance, ask the other person what they think of the music or the kind of music they like. If you are at a non-franchise restaurant and are waiting in line with someone else, ask what he or she thinks of the restaurant's food and whether he or she has any recommendations.

This type of ritual question can be combined with the first type of ritual question, particularly if you are at a movie theater or bookstore. Asking what someone is reading is an excellent conversation starter, as is asking if the bookstore or movie theater is the best one in the area.

Another way to use this type of ritual question is to offer assistance to someone, provided that they need it. Mention that they look as though they need help first, then offer your assistance. As an example, say you live in an apartment complex and you see someone unpacking his or her car and taking suitcases into the complex. You could say, "I noticed you looked like you needed some help unpacking your car. I live in this apartment complex. Would you like me to help you out?" Alternately, you could start by asking if he or she is a new tenant and say, "I happen to live here, too. Let me help you with unloading, and I can tell you about the complex while we are working."

If you cannot think of anything else, a ritual question good in any situation is to ask someone whether they are new in the area. This results in a good conversation starter because you can then ask them how long they have lived in the area or what brought them there.

The third kind of ritual question is to focus on something interesting about the other person. This is one of the most useful types of ritual questions because it could be anything: the latest smartphone model, a nice piece of clothing or dress, or a hairstyle. This ritual question is sure to get anyone talking to you as long as you start with a compliment. Unfortunately, a question about something can be perceived as a compliment or insult, and the reaction of people who are not sure why you are asking about something is to give a guarded response. A compliment gives the other person a clear signal that you like whatever it is you have noticed and that you are interested in learning more.

Some ritual questions, based on the above points of interest, could go as follows:

- "You have a smartphone. I have wanted one of those. What is the best advantage to having that particular model?"

- "That is such a nice dress. Where did you buy it?"

- "I like your tie. Where did you get it?"

- "That is a nice hairstyle. How long did it take to get it done?"

All these questions, in addition to taking less than 10 seconds to ask, have another thing in common — they are open-ended. They cannot be answered by a simple "yes" or "no," the way close-ended ritual questions can.

Here are some sample open-ended questions:

- What is the best part of that book you are reading?

- What was the first song you ever heard by your favorite band?

- How far in advance do you prepare your income taxes?

- What is your favorite radio station?

- What is the best nightclub in the city?

- What is your favorite movie?

- What is the geekiest thing you have ever done?

- Have you ever gotten involved as a volunteer in an election?

- How did you get your job?

- What was the last concert you went to?

- Where would you most like to travel?

- What is the most radical change you have made to your hair?

- What is your favorite kind of ride at an amusement park?

- What is the best sightseeing attraction in the United States?

If you are not used to holding a conversation, you might feel you are intruding on someone by asking an open-ended question. In truth, however, people like sharing information about themselves. It makes them feel important. Also, people can give an indication of how willing they are to talk when they answer these questions. If someone gives short answers even if you ask an open-ended question, it is a clear signal that he or she does not want to talk. On the other hand, if someone gives a long answer to a close-ended question, you can rest assured that he or she would like to talk with you.

Abstract and Concrete Language

If you feel you are saying the wrong thing when trying to instigate a conversation, adjust your language to be more concrete. Abstract language, which refers to principles and ideas without being specific, can be confusing when two people do not share common experiences. For example, if you ask someone you just met whether he or she wants to hang around, you will get a lukewarm response or an outright rejection. This is because you are using language that is too abstract. On the other hand, if you ask a friend if he or she wanted to hang out, he or she would know what the two of you do when you hang out, such as playing ping-pong or watching B-movies and having pizza.

Using concrete language and specific examples is the best way to overcome this hurdle. Instead of asking someone if they want to do something fun, specify what it is you have in mind. For instance, "I was thinking of playing some Frisbee, then walking down to the ice cream booth and getting some ice cream," is a specific example that will get someone interested, even if they do not like ice cream.

HELLO, MY NAME IS...

At some point in the conversation, you are going to need to introduce yourself. This is not easy information to work into a conversation, which is ironic when you think about how important a name is to someone.

Introducing yourself at the start of a conversation is acceptable, but it can be awkward. There are few good segues from an introduction to a conversation topic, and it smacks of the elementary school greeting, "Hi, my name is so-and-so. Will you be my friend?" A child can get away with that kind of honest desperation, but as an adult, you cannot be that emotionally open with a stranger.

The best way to introduce yourself is to do it early on in the conversation, when it is your turn to speak. After the other person has finished, say, "By the way, my name is..." and tell them. The other person will introduce himself or herself in return, and then you can get back to the topic at hand.

Once you get someone's attention, you have 20 seconds to keep it. What do you say after the initial back-and-forth talk of open-ended and close-ended questions? And what do you say when the other person asks you an open-ended question in return? This section is going to walk you through the transition from introductory conversation into full-on small talk, including when to switch from small talk to more personal conversation.

Why make small talk?

Small talk starts with the first round of introductory questions and answers, and it continues until the point where one party starts to deepen the conversation by revealing some personal details. People tend to look down on small talk and see it as a barrier to getting to know people, but it is a useful tool to have in your communications portfolio. Making small talk encourages the meaningful kinds of conversation people are hungry for in several ways.

First, small talk serves as a social litmus test for whether a person wants to talk or not. If a person answers a question in short sentences or with "yes" or "no" answers, he or she is not interested in talking with you.

Once people in a conversation have signaled that they want to talk, small talk lets you and the other person feel each other out and determine whether you want to talk to the person, and once you have decided to continue the conversation, exchange basic information about yourselves. In the process, you can establish what common ground you have. In the course of revealing this information, you are also likely to reveal topics that you are interested in, and if you listen carefully, you can tell what those topics are and talk about them in the course of the conversation. Small talk is a gateway drug to meaningful conversations people dream of having.

Listen to me

One of the fears of making small talk with someone is that you will have nothing to say. There you are, listening to someone talk about the goatherd his grandmother has, and when he or she finishes, you realize you have no idea what to say back. What can you say in return that you and he or she will find relevant?

If you find yourself in this situation, you were suffering from a fairly common conversational affliction — not paying attention to what the other person was saying. Instead, the moment he or she started talking about the goatherd, you thought to yourself, "So his grandmother has a goat herd. What do you say to someone who's just said that his grandmother has a goatherd?" Instead of listening to what your new friend had to say, you had focused all your attention on worrying about what to say, leaving you at a loss when it was your turn to speak. This is common with shy or scared people, so if this has happened to you, do not worry. Learn to listen actively to pick up on pieces of information you can use to continue the conversation.

Active listening is a part of making small talk. When you listen actively, you are signaling that you are taking the conversation and the other people in it seriously. They will participate more in the conversation as a result, and everyone will benefit.

Part of active listening comes from practicing good body language. Leaning forward, maintaining eye contact, and nodding to show you understand what is being said. The other part of active listening has to do with knowing what you are listening for.

The first step in being an active listener is making a conscious effort to become one. When talking with someone, tell yourself you are going to actively listen to him or her. Remind yourself you are going to focus on the information he or she is giving to you. That will put you in the correct frame of mind.

Second, eliminate background noise. No matter who you are talking to, having a conversation is easier when there is no background noise interfering with your ability to listen and your thought process. Loud music, television, and other conversations can distract you from the person you on whom you are supposed to be concentrating. To cut down on background noise, try to find a quieter area. This is not possible, like when you are in a nightclub and trying to speak over the music. In this situation, the best thing you can do is to have a starter conversation and then arrange to continue the conversation afterward. Related to background noise is physical stress. You will have a hard time paying attention to someone if you are tired.

Information trapping

While you are listening to someone else speak in a conversation, you will want to be aware of the personal information she is giving to you. The information can be used to discover what interests you have in common, then use those interests to carry on the conversation.

Be on the alert for these types of personal information:

- Hobbies
- Favorite sports teams
- Family members
- Friends
- Their job
- What kind of car is owned
- Books they like to read
- Recent movies they have watched
- Exercise habits
- Favorite food
- Where they live
- Neighbors
- Goals
- College attended
- Pets
- Religion
- Political affiliation

These items are a sampling of personal information that someone will reveal about himself or herself in a conversation.

When someone reveals information that you want them to talk about further, ask a question about what they were saying. Journalists refer to this as asking a follow-up question, and while an interviewee might not like being pressed for information, the people you are talking with will.

The best follow-up questions to ask are open-ended. This keeps the attention firmly on the person you are talking to, and lets him or her know you are interested in what he or she has to say. You can also use a close-ended question if he or she says something you do not understand or that seems unclear. A close-ended type of question also lets your conversation partner know you are listening, but too many close-ended questions in a row can appear you are grilling him, or that you were not paying close attention.

CASE STUDY: GETTING OVER YOUR EX AND STARTING TO MOVE ON

As a licensed psychotherapist in southern California with more than 30 years of counselling experience and the author of 13 books on relationships, Dr. Tina Tessina has earned her alias as "Dr. Romance." Here she shares some advice on spending time with your ex and getting ready to move on. While her advice is aimed at people going through a divorce, her advice is also useful to anyone whose relationship has failed. If your ex is mean or belligerent toward you, Dr. Tessina recommends keeping a cool head and following this set of guidelines:

Choose your battles. One of my clients once said, "I don't want to die on that hill." She meant, "That battle isn't worth what it will cost me;

I'll ignore that problem and save it for a bigger one." Do not get into adversarial positions with your ex when it is not necessary. Even if he or she drives you crazy, do not be oppositional. Save your energy for the big issues.

Do not react, respond. Think carefully about what you say before you say it. Calculate your words to get the response you want from your ex, rather than creating a problem you will have to clean up later. It works better to deal with difficult exes by phone message or e-mail, rather than in person. Everyone stays calmer.

Leave it in the divorce court. You have fought your battle. It came out however it did, now let it go. You once chose this partner, and you have things to learn about your choices. Focus on learning your lessons, and do not re-fight the old battles that are already settled. Do your part in the custody agreement, and if he or she does not do his or hers, keep a diary of all the times he or she did not. If he or she creates scenes, quietly listen and tape-record them. If you get a nasty phone message, tape it and save it. You can bring all this evidence to your lawyer to take to court and win your battles there.

As you go through the grieving process, Dr. Tessina has five pieces of advice to help you move on emotionally:

1. If you gave it your best shot and you know it is over, do not waste time in resentment and anger; it is self-destructive. Let go. Do your grieving, cry, journal, and talk about it with a trusted friend. Have a "letting go" ceremony with close friends, and say goodbye to your married life. Put reminders away for a while.

2. Do not hesitate to get therapy to help you through this transition, so you can grieve what is lost (even if you are the one who left, you have lost your hopes and dreams for this marriage) and move your focus on building a good life in your new circumstance. A professional viewpoint will help you move from past to present and plan for the future.

3. Take care of yourself financially — a good lawyer can help you fight for your rights. You will feel less resentment if you get your fair share of the assets.

4. This is an important time to have your friends or family around you; you need support. Do not isolate. You do not have to go right out and

date again — go slow — but have a social life with friends and family. Even if you do not think you feel ready to see people, see your closest friends and spend time with them. They will help you heal and will remind you that you still have people who love you. Spend time with people you trust.

5. Focus on building your life. This is a time to try something other than a relationship — take a class, start a new business or career, or get a puppy. Give yourself time to heal before taking another chance on love.

Last, as you end the grieving process, keep in mind Dr. Tessina's recommendations on how to let go of the pain the dissolution of your relationship has caused.

If your marriage ends in divorce, you lose more than the marriage. Even if your marriage had problems, or you were the one who wanted out, you still will have grief over the dreams and hopes that have died with the relationship. The overwhelming feeling of loss can be confusing and difficult to understand. The following tips will help you move through these feelings and begin to focus on the future.

1. Get support: The people around you will express conflicting feelings because they are experiencing shock and loss, too. This might be a time when you find out who your true friends are. Some of your friends will avoid dealing with you or choose your ex. You need trusted friends, family, and a church or support group who will care about you, listen to you, and not judge or try to get you to "get over it."

2. Talk or write it out: Talk and write until you have expressed your grief, loss, anger, confusion, and disappointment. Assume you have a specific number of tears to shed, and the more you express your feelings, the quicker you will come to the end of tears. Expressing your grief might be more than your support system wants to hear. A support group, clergy person, or therapist will be able to listen without judging until you have said everything you need to say.

3. Have a ceremony: When you feel ready, create a ceremony for letting go of your grief. You might want to include some of your close friends, destroy a memento that symbolizes your grief or the lost relationship, and share your hopes for the future.

Finding common interests

You can ask almost anything you want, but the best questions to ask are on subjects the other person feels passionately about and about interests they have in common with you. Discussing common interests forms an instant bond between you and the other person. It is also a ready-made topic for small talk. You can easily spend a conversation talking about one interest both of you share.

Conversations also run smoother if everyone involved is talking about a topic that interests them. Think back to a time you have had a successful conversation with someone. Odds are that you were discussing a topic with the other person that you felt strongly about or enjoyed. You were not worrying about whether the person you were talking with found you interesting or how to keep the conversation going. New topics based on that common interest presented themselves naturally, and you and the other person smoothly segued from one aspect of your common interest to the next with as much ease as walking. Talking about your passions is easier than talking about subjects you are unfamiliar with.

What do you do with the information once you have it?

Now you know something about the person with whom you are talking. You know where he or she lives, does for a living, and maybe even a hobby or two. You might also be wondering what to do with this information now that you have it.

The answer is simple: Learn more about the person. Take one of the topics or pieces of personal information you have learned and ask the other person about it. At this stage of the conversation, pick and choose a topic that interests you, and have options available. Ask open-ended questions about what you have learned and throw in close-ended questions for clarification.

The Building Blocks of a Romantic Relationship

Most romantic relationships begin the same way friendly relationships do. People in close proximity to each other form bonds over time and progress from casual acquaintances to nascent friends and then stabilized friends. A romantic relationship, though, has three aspects working together that are not found in other kinds of relationships. These aspects mix together in different ways and create what are known as love styles, or ways that people express their love for each other.

The first aspect of a relationship is **passion**. A passionate relationship does not involve sexual passion, although that can play a part. Instead, passion is an intense desire for and positive feelings about the other person. It generates the emotional high you get when you fall in love with someone. Passion is responsible for the sparks in a relationship and the emotional highs you get from being in love. However, passion is inconstant. Passion ebbs and flows, and as a result, a relationship built on passion alone cannot last.

Commitment is a second aspect of the relationship and is the counterpart to passion. Although passion is a subconscious emotional decision that can come and go, commitment is a conscious choice. A decision to commit is based on the reward that continuing a relationship offers. The most common symbol of commitment is found in marriages, in particular, during the "for better or for worse" vows. Among the rewards committing to a relationship offers is the level of emotional support, the financial support, and the companionship the other person offers.

Underpinning passion and commitment is **intimacy**. When you feel intimate in a relationship, you feel close to the other person and a strong personal connection. Intimacy and passion are closely tied. When you feel passionate for someone, you also feel strongly about him or her, which increases feelings of intimacy. This is why passionate encounters are mistakenly assumed to generate more intimacy. However, intimacy does not ebb and flow as wildly as passion does. Intimacy is ongoing and abiding. It is the feeling that romantic partners have for each other even when they do not feel passionate. In addition, when you commit to a long-term relationship, you are consciously choosing to increase your intimacy with your partner.

Love styles

The importance that each of the three dimensions of love plays in an individual's perception of love varies. According to research John Alan Lee performed in 1973 and 1988, people express their love in one of three primary styles. Lee's research also uncovered secondary styles of how people express their love. These secondary styles are based on mixtures of the primary styles.

Eros love is the most passionate kind of love that can persuade you to ask out that cute person waiting in line behind you at the grocery store — it is intuitive and spontaneous. A person who expresses his or her love in the eros style falls in love with someone, and he or she falls hard. He or she expresses his or her love early on to his or her partner, and the intensity of their love transcends the physical aspects and easily encompasses spiritual and intellectual aspects of love.

A similar kind of primary love style is **ludus** love, which is more like a game to see whether you can get someone to fall in love with you and enjoy the feeling of falling in love with someone else. However, a deeper connection is not the ultimate aim of ludic love. Instead, the fun is in the chase, in playing the field. Ludic lovers are also more romantic. In a study that will shock no one, Clyde and Susan Hendrick discovered that men tend to express their love more ludically than women.

Women express their love more through the style of **storge**, the practical, sensible car in contrast to the exciting sports car that is erotic love. It is expressed gradually, and as opposed to the difficulties of erotic love, storgic love has a higher amount of stability and is more peaceful than eros love. This is perhaps the most common kind of love to come out of friendships because storgic love surfaces through discovering that you and your romantic partner have similar goals, enjoy similar things, and have similar values. Storgic love is not as intense as love in the eros style, but storgic love will not suffer the crashing conflicts that eros love can bring.

Another love style that women express is the **pragma** style of love, the first of the secondary love styles and the result of mixing storgic love with ludic love. Pragmatic lovers might seem cold and calculating at first because they have clear stipulations about with whom they fall in love. This type of love uses the storgic lover's sensibility and security and the strategizing ludic lovers use when playing the field. Pragmatic lovers believe that true, enduring love is the result of making sure partners are compatible before agreeing to fall in love. Pragmatic love is the foundation for an arranged marriage.

The polar opposite of pragma love is **mania** love, a love style you will see in most teenagers and a potent blending of eros and ludus styles. Low self-esteem fuels this love style, and a manic lover tends to be unsure if he or she is loved. The eros style of loving drives him or her to extreme highs and lows, while the ludic part of this love style leads him or her to evaluate a partner's love and commitment to him or her through games or tests. A manic lover can feel so strongly about his or her relationship that he or obsesses over it.

Last, there is **agape** love, a love that is considered so pure that people feel that it is unattainable. Agape love comes from two love styles — eros and storge — and means an agapic lover feels an intense passion toward his or her partner and feels this passion consistently. This kind of love is known for its selflessness and generosity. An agapic lover feels his or her best when his or her partner is happy and willingly ensures his or her partner is happy even if his or her efforts are not returned. Although purely agapic lovers are rare, people who express their love display agapic love to their partners.

Most people do not have one specific love style. Instead, they use a blend of primary and secondary love styles. Someone might be pragmatic when initially selecting a romantic partner and then be erotic throughout the relationship with a strong undercurrent of storgic stability. Also, love styles can change as people develop relationships and as they learn from previous ones. Your love style can also change as a result of your partner's love style. Your love style is not good or bad. What matters is how your love style connects with your partner's style.

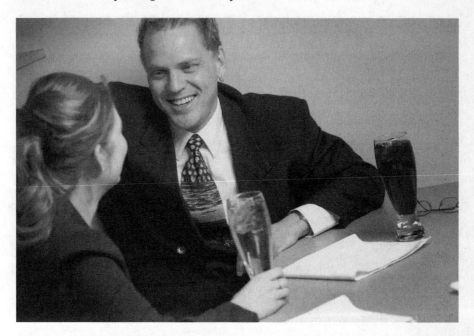

Mingling With Singles

Now that you know about love styles, you are ready to take on the singles scene in whatever part of the world you are in. You could be heading into the next hot nightclub, making your way through a trendy restaurant, sitting at an old-fashioned pub, or even going to a singles night at your local church or community hall.

When you go to a place to make new and potentially romantic connections, you are being as vulnerable as possible. According to conversation expert Debra Fine, no one likes to admit he or she is specifically looking to connect with someone. Starting a conversation with someone is easier if you have an excuse, such as being at a convention or a networking event. Despite this, talking with another single person is similar to talking with anyone else. The basic conversation techniques still apply, and it is just a matter of tweaking them to fit the situation.

Making your entrance

When you go to a singles event, do not feel you need to come in talking the first moment you enter the door. Instead, center yourself. Make sure you feel calm in whatever way works for you. Then, take one step through the door and, unless you are part of a line, stop and survey the situation. Be sure you continue to use relaxed, open body language. This will call attention to you, and it will also frame you as a self-confident person who is not afraid of attention. This will set you apart from the crowd, and it might entice people to come and talk with you instead of you having to make the first move.

After you have announced your presence, though, make an effort to blend in with the crowd. Do not feel you need to be the life of the party. Instead, wander through the crowd, and if there is a bar, get yourself something to drink. As you are doing so, get a sense of what the gathering is like. Are people excited or laid back? Does the mood seem formal or informal? Are people happy or stoic? Let your mind make observations, and then you can start turning those observations into icebreakers.

Impersonal icebreakers can be effective at singles events. Making an innocent remark about the event can spur someone to give his or her opinion of what is going on, and from there, you can use a ritual open-ended question to start a conversation.

How to Ask Someone On a Date

This is the whole reason you have been mingling with other singles. Someone has come along whom you connect with and who captivates you. You have talked with him or her for a while, and you want to make your move and ask him or her on a date.

For most people, this is the point where the mouth-and-brain connection fails completely. You want to ask this other person on a date in a way that is meaningful yet casual, sincere yet suave, and uses the right words so the other person will accept your offer. Also, there is the small matter that you are putting your ego on the line and risking the fact that you will be turned down, perhaps publicly, which is embarrassing. With that kind of pressure riding on the phrasing of one request, it is no wonder that many times people get tongue-tied. The best that they can come up with is, "Want to go out on a date next Saturday?" The main problem with this way of asking someone out is that, regardless of how much time you have spent talking to the other person, asking him or her out seems to come out of the blue, without any lead up.

When asking someone out on a date, do not ask the person if he or she wants to go out. Do not ask her what he or she is doing that Friday or Saturday night unless you have a fondness for hackneyed excuses, such as "Washing my hair." Instead, before you make the offer or call him or her on the phone, come up with some ideas about an activity this person might like to do. At this point, you might realize that to come up with these activities, actively listen to the person and keep at least a mental record of his or her likes, dislikes, personality, and hobbies. In other words, you need to use the skills you use in making friends if you want him or her to respond positively to your request for a date.

RUNNING OUT THE CLOCK

When you decide to ask someone on a date, there is the question of when you should do it. Some people immediately ask someone out on a date if the first meeting goes well. Others like to wait until the second or third meeting. Some even like to wait longer than that.

Asking someone out after you have met him or her multiple times is the best policy. This gives the person a chance to know you better and develop familiarity while there is still the excitement of meeting someone new. If you ask someone out on the first meeting, you are asking him or her to judge you as a romantic prospect, in addition to judging you as a person. If you wait too long, the excitement he or she feels will die down and leaving him or her less likely to see you as someone about whom he or she feels passionate.

However, do not feel pressured to ask someone out if you are not ready. If you need more time to get to know someone, do so. Good relationships come out of people knowing each other for a while before realizing there is an attraction.

If you are asked out

Congratulations. If someone has asked you on a date, he or she obviously thinks well of you. Enjoy the ego rush, and then accept or decline as you see fit. The only rule you need to follow is this: Empathize with the person who is asking you out. Do not lead him or her on, respond rudely, or act nonchalant. After all, the other person has taken a huge risk to confess his or her feelings to you. If you act nonchalant, the other person might get the impression that you do not care about him or her or the conversation. Neither will do his or her ego any good.

Instead, be enthusiastic if you accept his or her offer. If you cannot be enthusiastic, then show your interest in the upcoming date. If you decide to decline, let him or her down gently. He or she will be embarrassed, so try to convey that you are flattered and do not feel awkward about being asked out and that you might like to be friends anyway.

This advice applies no matter which gender you are. While women asking men out is becoming more common, a woman has to overcome the feeling of taking a huge risk and making herself vulnerable and also the difficulty of bucking a social norm. To do that takes courage. If nothing else, respect that courage.

Chapter 11

Meeting Your Match Online

It is exciting to think that you might stumble on the love of your life at any moment, yet, it is exhausting when it becomes apparent that no one around you is completely compatible with what you are looking for. It would be so much easier if you could just input all your likes and dislikes into the computer and have your ideal mate appear before your eyes, would it not?

The good news is that it is possible.

Online dating is an amazing resource. Nowhere else can you sift through a huge catalog of single people and contact the ones you like while you disregard the ones you do not. You do not have to get dressed up to search online for a potential date, and you can do it when it suits your schedule. That means that if the only time you have available to look for love is in the early morning before heading to work, you will still have the same options available to you if your schedule allows you to search on a Friday night. Online dating allows you to look for someone when it is convenient for you and in a way that also lets you be as selective as you like with whom you contact.

In a hectic world, online dating is the perfect solution to finding the love of your life.

Who and Why?

Who is online looking for love? The answer is simple: a wide variety of people. With online dating, you do not have to restrict your options to the singles living within your community or even within a hundred-mile radius of your home. Online dating allows you to expand your options to scour the globe in your search for love. The decision is yours. Do you want to find someone nearby, or are you willing to look all over the world? It is easy to meet single people with the specific geographic limitations of your choosing.

It does not stop with location. You can choose what kind of person you want to talk to depending on likes and dislikes, physical appearance, religious beliefs, and just about any other qualifying factors you might have. Are you looking for a tall, lanky person who is a Baptist and enjoys rollerblading? This person is online. Do you want to meet someone who is petite yet muscular, wealthy, and a strict vegetarian? If you log on to a dating site and enter these specifications, you will have different people from which to choose.

Why do people turn to online dating when trying to meet someone? Although everyone has different reasons for logging on to find potential dates, there are good reasons why this is a popular option.

People are busy. If you are working nine hours a day while also shouldering a long commute and everything else that comes with living as an adult, you do not have time to devote to finding a new relationship. You can choose to wait for potential mates to stumble into your life, but, if you are like most people, chances are you are a busy person and cannot spend time devoted to meeting new people. As culture turns toward an electronic age — texting, e-mailing, and social networking — you have found that people are turning to quick and efficient ways to meet others. After all, it is easier to sift through online dating profiles and shoot out a quick introductory e-mail than it is to wander through a bar and figure out how to get the attention of people who might or might not fit the mold of what you are looking for. Online dating simplifies the process for people who are too busy with life to meet people using traditional methods.

People are selective. You know what you are looking for, or at least you have an idea of what is acceptable in a mate and what is not. Online dating allows you to weed out the people who do not fit what you are looking for. Suppose you meet a person at a party and feel a connection to that person immediately. Will you feel comfortable enough to start listing your specific likes and dislikes? Imagine what an aggressive conversation that would be: "I need someone who can support themselves financially and who goes to a church with similar beliefs as my church has. Do you enjoy baseball? I cannot date a person who does not like Mexican food." The other person would feel violated by your barrage of questions and demands. With online dating, you can state your likes and dislikes before you ever make contact with another person. You can be as selective as you want without offending anyone.

People are curious. Many people wonder if it is possible to meet someone special online. They also wonder what type of people they will meet through a dating website. Commercials for popular dating sites make the claim that members are matched together using sophisticated technology, and for this reason, the perfect person is only mouse clicks away. Some people begin their online search as a result of sheer curiosity. "Who can I meet online? Is it possible to find someone special this way?" In some cases, these people are pleased to find they can meet people online, some of whom become lifelong friends and lifelong partners. Some online dating sites offer free peeks at compatible singles, and for many people, this peek is all they need to get intrigued enough to sign up and start meeting new people.

There are other reasons for turning to online dating. You, as someone who is recovering from a painful heartbreak, might feel intimidated by the prospect of returning to the dating scene. People might be interested in getting back into the swing of meeting new people and going on dates, yet have no idea how to go about it. For these people, online dating offers a safe way to reintegrate back into the singles scene without metaphorically going out on a limb. Searching through online profiles is not as intimidating as walking through a bar full of singles or asking friends to arrange a blind date.

With online dating, you can go at your own pace. You can decide to simply look through the other profiles or jump right in and post a profile and let people contact you. This is a fantastic way to meet other people and also maintain your acceptable comfort level.

Because many dating websites require membership fees, review which website is best for you before signing up. You might be anxious to jump right in and sign up for several websites at once, but it might be best to start with one or two websites and then decide if you want to add more sites into the mix. You might soon find that, while you like the format of one site, you prefer the type of singles that pop up on another; it will not take you long to settle into one particular website that suits your needs and is easy to use.

Location, Location, Location

Suppose you live in a small town or rural location where there are not many single people. This is a common scenario in smaller towns; everyone already knows one another, and if you do not find any available singles appealing, then you are out of luck. On the other hand, you might live in a large metropolitan area where people rush around and do not take the time to meet other people because they are too busy or are secure with their existing social circle. In either scenario, it can be difficult to meet prospective dates.

Online dating solves this problem. Location is an issue only if you want it to be when it comes to looking for someone online. On the other hand, online dating is not only suitable for people who have geographic restrictions. You might live in an area that has a bustling, thriving singles scene, but that does not mean you cannot benefit from meeting people online.

Real or Fake?

With many people online, it is safe to assume that no one tells the absolute truth on their profiles. While some people tell lies in an attempt to catch the eye of a potential mate — such as fibbing about age or not telling the entire truth when it comes to weight — there are people online who completely fabricate profiles with far cries from reality. For these people, online dating is amusement and is not an attempt to meet someone. Instead, perusing ads online and communicating with people is more an entertaining sport than anything else.

Take solace in the fact that these people are a tiny minority of the online dating population. The potential of bumping into one of these people online should not stop you from starting your online dating adventure. After all, when you walk into a singles bar, there is a chance you will meet someone who tells you a stream of lies, but this does not deter you from continuing your search.

The majority of people with profiles online put their profiles on websites because they have a genuine desire to meet someone new. Trust your intuition; if a profile seems fishy or fake, move on to the next one. Do not let the fear of a fake profile stop you from meeting the person of your dreams.

Nothing to Lose

Online dating offers an initial anonymity that you cannot get in the traditional dating scene. The ability to peruse databases of singles is like being able to walk through a bar without making yourself vulnerable. On the other side of the coin is the fact that there are no hurt feelings on the part of the people with profiles you glaze over because, in most cases, they do not even know that someone has looked and disregarded their profiles.

Online dating is a safe way to see what kinds of people are available. Because you are likely re-entering the dating scene after a long absence, perusing a database of singles can be a reassuring act. You will encounter a variety of potential partners, including attractive, accomplished people who will catch your eye and prove to you that there are still fish in the sea. If the database you look through does not contain anyone who appeals to you, there are other sites online that have databases full of people who might be right for you.

Dealing with backlash

Online dating is a mainstream practice and is becoming more common as a way to meet a mate. On the other hand, there are stigmas attached to online dating — especially among people who have not dated in today's society, such as grandparents and parents — that some people might be eager to point out to you once they find out you have a dating profile online.

If you tell people you are trying online dating, be prepared to get an earful of opinions. It is the people who have not tried online dating who are the same people who seem to have the most adamant opinions about online dating. Friends and family might tell you that online dating is for desperate people or that online dating is dangerous. People fear the things they do not understand, so take negative comments with a grain of salt.

As long as you are a single adult, you do not have to justify your foray into online dating to anyone. Your parents, friends, and the people you work with might have opinions. If you are older, your children might express their concerns that you are going to get taken advantage of by someone you meet online. Try to take everyone's concern as a compliment that they care about you, but do not feel you need to live your life to please anyone but yourself. The decision of whether to participate in online dating is up to you. You will learn that there are people online who are genuinely looking for a solid relationship with someone who is compatible with them and that the jerks and unstable people are the vast minority.

Which Site is Right For You?

Before you decide on one website or another, look at different sites and browse through them. Different sites offer different features. Do not be afraid to shop through sites, but settle down with one or two sites that have all the features you want and the type of people you are looking for.

Although you are likely familiar with popular dating sites, such as **www.eharmony.com**, **www.chemistry.com**, and **www.match. com**, there are some dating sites that are specific to a particular subculture. If you have specific likes and dislikes, look at dating sites that are specific to your wants and needs. For example, active duty military personnel live a demanding life and need someone who can understand this. For these people, a website, such as **www.militarysingles.com,** is a choice because it is specifically designed for military singles and the people who are interested in meeting them.

The same principle can be applied to other people with specific preferences. If you are looking to meet someone of the same gender, then you will find that, although some of the larger dating websites offer same-sex matches, there is a much larger selection to choose from by visiting a site like **www.gay.com**. Likewise, if you are Jewish and want to meet someone who is as well, it will be easier for you to find your match at **www.jdate.com**.

There are many dating websites that are dedicated to certain lifestyles and activities. Single parents can meet other single parents at **www.singleparentsmeet.com**. People who have been affected by cancer can meet other people in similar circumstances at **www.cisforcupid.com**. There is even a dating website specific to artists at **www.singleartistdating.com**.

Another example of websites catering to a certain population are those dedicated to certain religious beliefs. On sites like **www.christiansingles.com**, you will not find as many raunchy profiles as you would on a mainstream dating site. Although there are different denominations and levels of faith, people using a website like this are looking for like-minded singles who share similar values and a desire to date a Christian. You can specify your religious preferences on almost all the dating sites, but by subscribing to a site that is specifically designed for faith-based dating — such as **www.lutheranfriendfinder.com** (for Lutherans),

www.salaamlove.com (for Muslims), and **www.oldesouls.com** (for Pagans), you might be able to pinpoint a potential mate faster because you can assume that everyone registered on the site has similar beliefs as you do.

There is not one specific dating website that reigns supreme above others because there are many different people with varying tastes. The vast majority of dating websites are quite formulaic: You specify who you are and what you are looking for, and then you peruse eligible singles. You contact the ones you find appealing and reply to the singles who contact you. On the other hand, some websites are better than others. You will develop preferences about how you like to conduct a search for singles in a database and how you like information from a profile to be presented.

The best dating website is the one that you prefer above others. It should have a format that you find appealing and a database full of singles that have the potential to be compatible with you.

Chapter 12

Beginning a
New Relationship

I t is finally time. You might feel happy and confident enough on your own, but you would like to get in another relationship, not because you want to fill the void left by your previous relationship or are scared that if you do not find another date you will be the only person without someone else. You are looking for a relationship because you want to be in one.

Still, as the saying goes, once bitten, twice shy. Getting into a new relationship can be hard, especially if the last one broke your heart. You might have doubts about getting into a new relationship, such as whether the person you are dating will break your heart the same way your ex did, or you might find yourself wondering if you are over your ex. You are not alone. People experience these doubts when they start dating again.

Post-breakup Dating

The first date after a breakup can be odd, emotionally speaking. Even though you are trying to concentrate on how nice the other person is and the interesting story he or she is telling about when he or she scaled the Matterhorn, for some reason you realize you miss your ex, even though he or she did not scale anything higher than a stepladder. Here are some reactions relationship expert Susan Elliott compiled that you might have on your first post-breakup dates:

I am still mourning my old relationship

Grief is a funny thing. It can surface as a reaction to moving on and signal one last sense of loss as you turn the page. Other times, it can be a sign that you are still feeling the loss of your last relationship keenly enough that you should postpone dating longer. There is no test to determine which kind of grief it is. You need to figure it out for yourself, and it might take more than one date to figure it out. Any more than three dates, though, and you can be sure the feelings of grief are residual. If you feel the need to pull back, it is not because there is something wrong with you. You will be ready to date again. Just be patient.

I am not going to find someone

When you date someone, particularly if you are trying to make a good impression, start to become acutely aware of your shortcomings. Plus, dating is scary and difficult, no matter how nonchalant we try to be about it. This can overwhelm you, and then all you see is what is wrong — with yourself, with your date, and with the situation. When this happens, the important thing is to recognize it and take a mental step back. Excuse yourself to the restroom if you have to, and then give yourself a quick pep talk. *Repeating the affirmations you learned about in Chapter 5 is also recommended.*

I do not think this person likes me

If you get a sense that your date is not that into you, do not take it personally. If your date's rejection of you makes you feel bad, this might be a sign that you are not quite ready to start dating again. Give yourself a break from dating for a week or two, but look on the positive side — you had the courage to take that first step of getting back into the field.

I do not think I like this person

If you do not like your date, at least be gracious and do not end the date early unless he or she is being mean or obnoxious. After you get home, though, go through the date and try to discover what it was about the person you did not like. Is it because they shared some traits with your ex? Is it because they were different than your ex and you are out of your comfort zone? Whatever the reason, do not write off your date. You might even want to give him or her another chance, and if he or she is not for you, end things politely.

Standards and "Good Enough"

One of the problems with dating again is trying to figure out what you are looking for in a date. On the plus side, you have the experience you gained from your relationship with your ex, which should give you some perspective on what you are looking for. Your relationship with your ex is also on the negative side of the equation. If you like someone like your ex, does this mean that he or she will also break your heart the way your ex did?

As you start dating again, start evaluating your relationship with the person you are seeing. How much time do you spend together? How much time does he or she want to spend with you, versus the time you are comfortable with? How does your date react when you want to spend time with other people? These questions can be hard to ask, especially if you are lucky enough to have a date that goes well.

To properly assess how your date is going, spend time away from him or her. The best way to do that is to stick with your schedule. Keep appointments with your friends, continue working on your hobbies, and do not slack off on trips to the gym. While you are away from your new date and taking a breather from your emotions, consider what your boundaries are in this new relationship. What are you willing to compromise? What are the dealbreakers? How fast do you want this relationship to move? Once you have a sense of what you want out of this relationship, the next step is to stick to it. If your date wants you to move beyond your boundaries, politely but firmly refuse. This might lead to the end of your relationship, but in the long run, you need to be comfortable with yourself, and you are guaranteed to feel better when you refuse to compromise the principles that are important to you than you will be if you sacrifice them just to stay with someone. People in healthy relationships know what is important to them, and they know how to compromise without giving up anything important to them. You will have to practice to achieve this balance.

Standards can be too high. Do you only want to date people with salaries larger than $100,000 a year? Do you turn down people who do not look like bikini models? If so, loosen your standards. This does not mean you should completely abandon your standards, though. For instance, you want to date someone you are attracted to, and like it or not, looks do matter. When you assess whether you want to date someone, though, do not dismiss him or her if he or she does not look like a man or woman you would find in a magazine. The same rule applies if a potential date is not as financially well off as you would like.

OBLITERATING STANDARDS

If you want to shake up your dating world, you might try to follow in the footsteps of Maria Dahvana Headley. After realizing she seemed to date the same type of guys, she decided to do an experiment. For one year, she would go out with everyone who asked her out — no exceptions. Maria wrote about her experiences in a book, *The Year of Yes*, and detailed about her dates with playwrights, cowboys, salsa dancers, ice cream men, and how she eventually fell in love.

The opposite problem of having standards that are too high is accepting someone who is just "good enough." Everyone settles and compromises to some degree when forging a relationship, and that is to be expected. However, you do not want to be in a relationship with someone just because he treats you better than your ex did. By this point, you know what you want in a relationship, and you know what you are willing to compromise. You are worth having someone love you — without sacrificing what is important to you.

CASE STUDY: STRAIGHT TO THE POINT

Roy Biancalana is a relationship coach, the latest leg on a life journey that has seen him be the CEO of a nonprofit organization and a pro golfer. He has been trained by some of the top psychologists and relationship coaches in the country, and he is the author of A Drink with Legs: From Being Hooked to Being Happy — A Spiritual Path to Relationship Bliss.

Roy Biancalana is big on personal responsibility when it comes to the subject of breakups. "The first step is to feel your feelings deeply, allow it to be, and then let go of the victim mentality and take responsibility for how you contributed to the demise of the relationship. Understand that you break your own heart. You are responsible for your feelings."

One interesting aspect of Roy's philosophy behind breakups that stems from his mantra of personal responsibility is that people whose relationships fail are responsible for them. "You did this to yourself; you wanted out of the relationship — and we know that because that is what happened." This straightforward attitude differs considerably from other relationship coaches' advice.

How does this philosophy translate into counseling someone after they have gone through a breakup? "The advice I give is to tell the complete truth," Roy says. "Own your part in the relationship, let go of playing the victim, which means to stop blaming, complaining, judging, or labeling (your ex). If you have awakened to your own personal issues that contributed to the entire relationship and its demise — and shifted around those unconscious beliefs — then you would have no trouble or fear of opening your heart, for you are no longer the same person and cannot therefore create a similar result."

When dealing with an ex, Roy prefers to look past how people should act and focus on what is going on. "I don't deal in 'shoulds,'" he explains. "If (someone whose relationship has failed) is mean and nasty, then it is simply a sign that they are playing the victim and seeing the ex as a villain. If you see yourself as the victim and the ex as the villain, you will try to get your children — and everybody else — on your side and turn them against your ex. When they see that they wanted the relationship to end, unconsciously, all anger and meanness dissolves by itself. And when a person goes through a breakup, they wanted it on some level."

Roy has the same no-nonsense approach when it comes to being able to date again. "Time tables are silly. You are ready to start dating when you unwind your responsibility for the breakup and when you no longer feel attachment or aversion toward your ex. That can happen within days; for others, it does not happen for decades. You have to know your issues and shift them or you will attract the same kind of person and create the same kind of relationship. So they should approach dating with fear if they have not done their work, but joy if they have."

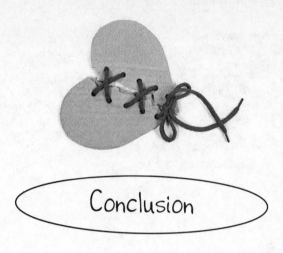

Conclusion

You are finally here. Congratulations. It has not been an easy journey, but you have gotten through your grief and accepted that your old relationship has ended. You feel good about yourself, and although you might not be completely satisfied with where you are in life, you are happy with where you are and you have some goals toward which you are working.

You are stronger than you were when you first began the book. Remember the old saying, "What doesn't kill you makes you stronger?" You have officially joined the ranks of those strengthened by adversity.

Now get out on the dating scene and enjoy yourself.

Bibliography

Baxter, Leslie. *Encyclopedia of Human Relationships*. By Harry T. Reis and Susan Sprecher. Thousand Oaks, CA: SAGE Publications, 2009. N. pag. Print.

Behrendt, Greg, and Amiira Ruotola-Behrendt. *It's Called a Breakup Because It's Broken: the Smart Girl's Breakup Buddy*. New York: Broadway, 2005. Print.

Bronson, Howard F., and Mike Riley. *How to Heal a Broken Heart in 30 Days: a Day-by-day Guide to Saying Goodbye and Getting on with Your Life*. New York: Broadway, 2002. Print.

"Divorce Source: Children & Divorce: The Different Age Stages." *Divorce Source: a Legal Resource for Divorce, Custody, Alimony, and Support*. N.p., n.d. Web. 31 Aug. 2010. **www.divorcesource.com/info/children/stages.shtml**.

Elliott, Susan J. *Getting past Your Breakup: How to Turn a Devastating Loss into the Best Thing That Ever Happened to You.* Cambridge, MA: Da Capo Lifelong, 2009. Print.

"The Four Stages of Grief: Denial." *Relationships, Relationship Advice, Relationship Problem Advice, Emotional Intimacy.* N.p., n.d. Web. 01 Sept. 2010. **www.couplescompany.com/Features/Grief/ Denial.htm**.

"Parenting Issues for Unmarried Couples FAQ - *Divorce & Family Law Center." Divorce, Child Custody, Child Support, Marriage, Adoption - FindLaw Family Law Center.* N.p., n.d. Web. 31 Aug. 2010. **http://family.findlaw.com/living-together/living-together-basics/unmarried-parenting(1).html**.

Phillips, Stacy D. "What to Do When Your Ex-Spouse Threatens You or Your Family." *Divorce 360.* N.p., 21 May 2008. Web. **www.divorce360.com**.

Piderman, Katherine. "Forgiveness: Letting Go of Grudges and Bitterness - MayoClinic.com." *Mayo Clinic Medical Information and Tools for Healthy Living - MayoClinic.com.* N.p., n.d. Web. 31 Aug. 2010. **www.mayoclinic.com/health/forgiveness/MH00131**.

Stosny, Steven. "Mad about You: Simple and Complex Jealousy | Psychology Today." *Psychology Today: Health, Help, Happiness Find a Therapist.* N.p., n.d. Web. 01 Sept. 2010. **www.psychologytoday.com/blog/anger-in-the-age-entitlement/201002/mad-about-you-simple-and-complex-jealousy**.

W, Bill. *The A.A. Service Manual ; Combined With, Twelve Concepts for World Service.* New York, NY. Alcoholics Anonymous World Services, 1987. Print.

Williams, Julia. "Relationship Advice for the Bitter Single Person." *Associated Content* N.p., n.d. Web. 01 Sept. 2010. **www.associatedcontent.com/article/220062/relationship_advice_for_the_bitter.html?cat=72**.

Author Biography

Chris Gottschalk is a Michigan native who currently lives in northeast Iowa. When he is not writing, Chris is reading, exercising, swimming, cooking, traveling, and terrorizing all bookstores in a 60-mile radius.

Index

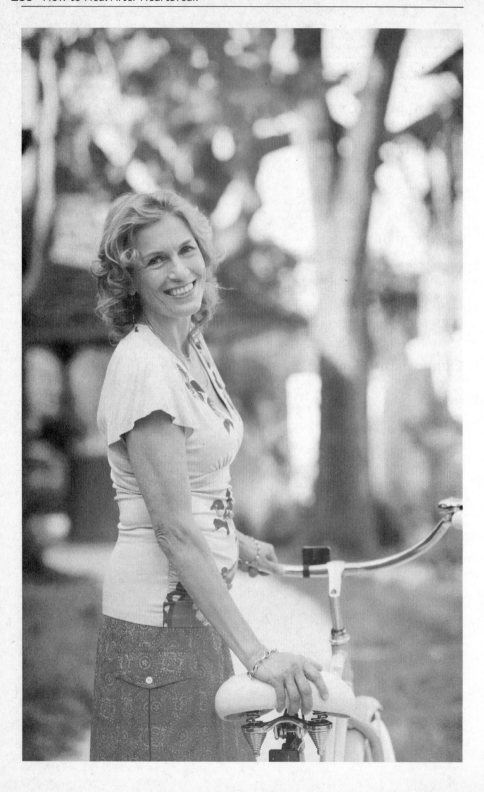